a Heart Like His

EDITATIONS on the
ACRED HEART OF JESUS

THOMAS D. WILLIAMS

Cover and interior design by Rule 29 Creative | www.rule29.com

Scripture texts in this work (unless otherwise noted) are taken from the *New
Revised Standard Version Bible,* copyright 1989, Division of Christian
Education of the National Council of the Churches of Christ in the
United States of America. All rights reserved.

Imprimi Potest:
Julio Martí, LC

Library of Congress Cataloging-in-Publication Data

Williams, Thomas D., LC.
A heart like his : June meditations on the Sacred Heart of Jesus /
Thomas D. Williams.
p. cm.
ISBN 978-1-933271-34-7
1. Sacred Heart, Devotion to--Meditations. I. Title.

BX2157.W55 2010
242'.2--dc22

2010008584

Printed in the United States of America

10 9 8 7 6 5 4 3 2 1

table of contents

An introduction

I don't know about you, but I get a little squeamish when it comes to devotion to "body parts." Relics are one thing, but "body parts" are another. Living in Italy for the last eighteen years, I have gotten somewhat accustomed to the practice, but one's initial uneasiness never disappears altogether.

Here in Rome, for instance, at the church of Santa Maria Sopra Minerva we have the incorrupt body of St. Catherine of Siena. Well, most of her body, that is, since her head was removed and sent back to her native Siena, along with a finger, for display at the church of St. Dominic. We also have St. Francis Xavier's right forearm, though the rest of him is apparently exhibited in the Basilica of Bom Jesus in Goa, India. Across town, we have the Capuchin Church of the Immaculate Conception, familiarly known as the "Bone Church," since the crypt below it is entirely decorated in the bones of deceased Capuchins. The list goes on and on...

Relics or realities?

So isn't there something strange about us modern men and women in the twenty-first century reading a book about devotion to the "Sacred Heart" of Jesus? At worst, isn't this just more worship of "body parts," and at best, isn't it a quaint scrap of dusty piety left over from our great-grandparents' day? Shouldn't we be moving on to something a little more trendy, a little more hip, and a little less "earthy"? Odd as it may seem, devotion to the Sacred Heart is not just some back-alley practice for the macabre-minded. Nor is it an outdated vestige of medieval piety to be quietly brushed under the rug. It was none other than Pope Benedict XVI who recently said that devotion to the Sacred Heart "has an irreplaceable importance for our faith and for our life in love."[1]

In explaining this devotion, Pope John Paul II similarly made clear that the Heart of Christ is not just a physical organ, like the pancreas or the gallbladder. When we speak of the heart, he said, we refer to "our whole being, all that is within each one of us."

---

1   Letter of Pope Benedict XVI, *To the Most Reverend Father Peter-Hans Kolvenbach, S.J,* May 15, 2006.

The heart represents "all that forms us from within, in the depths of our being. All that makes up our entire humanity, our whole person in its spiritual and physical dimension."[2]

Unlike the head (symbol of rational thought and calculation) or the belly (symbol of visceral desire), the human heart represents the seat of principles, decisions, convictions, yearnings, commitments, aspirations, and love. Devotion to the Sacred Heart of Jesus, then, means devotion to Jesus himself, to the Word made flesh, to the humanity of the Son of God, and, in a particular way, to the love of God in human form.

Knowing about Jesus or knowing Jesus?

Knowing Jesus Christ means more than knowing when and where he lived, or what he said and did. It means getting to know him more intimately by penetrating into his heart. Knowing him, in turn, leads to loving him, to entering into a friendship with him, and that leads to imitation. But imitating Jesus likewise means more than outward mimicking of his

---

2   Pope John Paul II, Homily at Abbotsford Airport (Vancouver), Tuesday, September 18, 1984.

actions. It means allowing the Holy Spirit to make our hearts more like his.[3]

That, in short, is the whole point of this devotion. The simple meditations I offer in this volume are meant to help Christians in this endeavor: to know Christ more intimately, to love him more profoundly, and to imitate him more perfectly.[4]

As a standard for our own behavior, we often ask: What would Jesus do? This is a key question, but I can't help thinking that many times, our answer reflects "what I would do if I were Jesus," rather than "what Jesus would do if he were in my place." Why is this? Surely it's not ill will—it must rather

---

3   *"Following Christ* is not an outward imitation, since it touches man at the very depths of his being. Being a follower of Christ means *becoming conformed to him* who became a servant even to giving himself on the Cross. Christ dwells by faith in the heart of the believer, and thus the disciple is conformed to the Lord. This is the *effect of grace*, of the active presence of the Holy Spirit in us" (Pope John Paul II, encyclical letter *Veritatis Splendor*, no. 21).

4   "Is not a summary of all our religion and, moreover, a guide to a more perfect life contained in this one devotion [to the Sacred Heart]? Indeed, it more easily leads our minds to know Christ the Lord intimately and more effectively turns our hearts to love Him more ardently and to imitate Him more perfectly"(Pope Pius XI, encyclical letter *Miserentissimus Redemptor*, May 8, 1928, AAS XX, 1928, p. 167).

be from ignorance. We simply don't know Jesus as well as we should.

Becoming like Jesus means becoming more human and more holy. What is holiness after all except union with God, a union that passes through the humanity of Christ and perfects our own humanity? The Second Vatican Council reminded us that Christ "reveals man to man himself... He who is 'the image of the invisible God' is himself the perfect man." Moreover, "by his incarnation, the Son of God has united Himself in some fashion with every man. He worked with human hands, he thought with a human mind, acted by human choice, and loved with a human heart."[5]

If we want to know who *we* are, who we were created to be, we will find the answer in Jesus Christ and especially in his *heart*. This is a down-to-earth devotion, not based on esoteric practices or special techniques, but on contemplation of Jesus Christ, who reveals God to us and reveals our true selves as well.

---

5   Second Vatican Council, Pastoral Constitution on the Church in the Modern World *Gaudium et Spes,* no. 22.

giving god a chance to change our hearts

Union with Christ is not just the result of hard work either. We grow more and more like Christ by cooperating with his grace in our lives.[6] In order to grow in faith and love we Christians need to *experience* the love of Christ. We need to see it, feel it, grasp it, be overwhelmed by it, immerse ourselves in it. Only the intense experience of being unconditionally loved—by none other than God himself—can enable us to love him and others as we yearn to.

St. John wrote that love consists in this, "not that we have loved God, but that he has loved us" (1 Jn 4:10). We need, in Pope John Paul's words, *to penetrate the heart of Christ.*[7] And as Pope Benedict recently wrote, it is by deepening our relationship with the heart of Jesus that "we will be able to understand better what it means *to know* God's love in Jesus Christ, *to experience* him, keeping our gaze fixed on him to

---

6   To imitate and live out the love of Christ is not possible for man by his own strength alone. He becomes *capable of this love only by virtue of a gift received.* (VS 22)

7   "No one can truly know Jesus Christ well without penetrating his Heart, that is, the inmost depths of his divine and human Person" (Pope John Paul II, *Angelus* message, June 20, 2004).

the point that we *live* entirely on the experience of his love, so that we can subsequently *witness* to it to others."[8]

In the following pages, then, I will offer thirty meditations, one for each day of the month of June, the month traditionally dedicated to the Sacred Heart of Jesus. I also include two extra meditations to be used on the feasts of the Sacred Heart of Jesus and the Immaculate Heart of Mary respectively. Each meditation will focus on one particular aspect or virtue of the heart of Christ, as seen in the Gospel. I would hope to offer as comprehensive a view as possible of the many facets of his heart, so that at month-end we will know, love, and imitate him a little better. For some the book may serve as a short daily reading, as something to think about and reflect on during the day. For others, it will provide material for a period of prayer, to meditate on Jesus' love and converse with him in the depths of your heart.

Our goal, as I have said, is to know Jesus so as to love him and then imitate him. Day after day, our prayer will be: *Lord, let*

---

8   Letter of Pope Benedict XVI, *To the Most Reverend Father Peter-Hans Kolvenbach, S.J*, May 15, 2006.

me know you so well that I cannot help but love you. Let me love you so deeply that I cannot help but want to be like you. Make my heart more like yours!

JUNE I

A **humble** HEART

*"Learn from me, for I am meek
and humble of heart."*

Mt 11:29

There is no more "classic" virtue of the heart of Christ than his humility. This is Jesus' own doing, since he expressly invited his followers to imitate him with these words: "Come to me all you who are weary and find life burdensome and I will refresh you. Shoulder my yoke and learn from me, for I am meek and humble of heart, and you will find rest for your souls."

What image, experience, or association comes to mind when I think of the word "humility"? Does the concept attract or repel me? Why?

These are some of the most heartening and consoling words in the whole Gospel. It is hard to read them without feeling lifted up and comforted. Jesus promises rest and refreshment for our souls, and who doesn't need that? But the path to get there might not be quite so clear. What does it mean to "shoulder his yoke" and to learn to be "meek and humble"? What about people with strong, "alpha" temperaments? Are they called to be meek and humble too, or is there another way?

Reading through the Gospel, we see that Jesus never put on airs. He didn't care what other people thought of him. He didn't crave others' attention, or worry about impressing them. He always spoke the truth but he didn't spend time arguing with people out of a need to have to be right. He just went about doing good and fulfilling the mission he was sent to carry out. In fact, it seems that Jesus didn't spend much time thinking about himself at all. He was always either praying or teaching or helping others or healing. And he did so as a gift to others with no strings attached.

To say that Jesus was "meek" and "humble" certainly doesn't mean he was a wimp or a milksop. If anyone had a

In which of my relationships do I tend to "lord it over" others? Why?

strong character, he did. He was a true leader, with clear ideals and convictions and an iron will. Yet at the same time he had time for the "little people," for beggars, poor people, children, prostitutes and tax men. He never acted superior to the people he was with but listened to their problems and came to their assistance. He knew that he was "Lord" and yet he never "lorded" it over anyone.

Even when performing his miracles, we never see Jesus with a "look at me" attitude. He calls his miracles "signs"—signs that he is who he says he is, so that people will listen to his message of salvation. In fact, when the people are so overwhelmed by Jesus' multiplication of loaves that they want to carry him off to make him king, he quietly slips away to pray (Jn 16:15). He isn't after their accolades. All he wants is to show them the path to salvation.

The same humility that Jesus shows toward other people we see in his interactions with God, his Father. He seems averse to taking credit for anything, and refers everything back to the Father. Jesus once said to his apostles that when they had done everything they were supposed to do, they should say, "We are useless servants. We have done no more than our duty" (Lk 17:10). That's exactly what Jesus does. In similar fashion, Jesus doesn't profess to be "original" or "innovative" but says that all his teaching comes from what he learned from the Father (cf. Jn 7:16). In a world where people scramble to claim credit for everything they do, Jesus provides a refreshing example of disinterested service.

———— ✦ ————

So what about us? How are we called to be more like him? Humility is a funny virtue, because we love it in other people but have a tough time practicing it ourselves. It hurts so much when people humiliate us, or forget about us, or don't take our opinions into account. We like— almost *need*—to be appreciated. We sometimes feel sorry for ourselves and often compare ourselves to others (sometimes feeling superior, other times envious, other times bitterly inferior). The point is, if we are honest, we find a lot of *pride* in ourselves that we don't see in Jesus (and if we don't recognize it in ourselves, we are worse off still!).

Yet Jesus promises that the yoke of humility is sweet. When we embrace it, we find "rest for our souls"!

Lord, help me to be honest with myself, and honest with you. There are so many things in my heart that need repairing if I am to be like you. I really do want other people to see you in me, and I know that in order for that to happen I must forget about myself. I must become more humble. I really do want to grow to be more like you, Jesus. How beautiful it would be if the one thing I could be known for is my resemblance to you!

Help me to love humility, Lord. Let me not fear humiliations, since I know how much you love me and that should be enough. All I have is what you have given me, so what is there for me to be vain about? Rather, let me be grateful for my gifts and put them all at the disposal of others and of your kingdom.

Use my intelligence, my health, my communications skills, my sense of humor, my strength, my special talents, and even my

17

weaknesses and faults to bring others to you. Help me not to be harsh or off-putting with others; you never were. Let people find in me—as they found in you—an open heart, a welcoming smile, and a listening ear.

———◆◆◆———

Jesus, meek and humble of heart,
make my heart more like yours!

JUNE 2

A **thirsty** HEART

"Give me to drink."
Jn 4:7

We (rightly) think of God as our provider. He is the go-to guy, the one who has everything. He has all the answers. He has the strings of the universe in his hands. He is all-knowing, all-powerful and all-encompassing. So it's natural that we have a tough time coming to grips with Jesus as a beggar, as one who experiences need. These needs can be as basic as hunger or thirst but also go much deeper.

Jesus says that whoever gives a Christian a cup of cold water to drink will not lose his reward (see Mt 10:42). He says that whenever someone gives drink to a thirsty person, he considers it done for him (see Mt 25:37-40). But he also expresses his own thirst, both on the cross (see Jn 19:28) and in dealing with others. Perhaps the most poignant example of this is with the encounter with the Samaritan woman at Jacob's well in Sychar (Jn 4:4-42).

How deeply do I believe that I have something God wants?

Jesus is sitting by the well around noon, when a Samaritan woman approaches to draw water. Of all the possible ways Jesus could open a conversation with her (which was already strange enough, since Jews didn't speak to Samaritans, especially a woman), Jesus makes a request. He doesn't offer salvation or teach about the Kingdom of God, at least not right away. He asks for a drink of water. It is a logical request, of course, on a hot summer's day in Palestine. Still, we expect Jesus to offer something rather than ask for something. What does this mean?

Let's take a step back for a moment. By making us free, God accepted the fact that he no longer would have everything in his control. He can move mountains, change tides, and create and destroy universes—but he cannot make us love him. He needs to ask for our love, in hopes that we will respond. This is very frightening if we think of the awesome responsibility it gives us. As scary as this may be, however, it is actually wonderful news for Christians. The saddest thing imaginable would be that our love didn't matter to God, that he didn't care. Imagine experiencing the tremendous love of God and not being able to give him anything in return! But we can. We can give him things that he doesn't have: our faith, our trust, our love.

Jesus thirsts, all right, but he doesn't just thirst for water. His heart thirsts for souls. He thirsts for love. We mustn't think that this thirst is the expression of some narcissistic need to be loved, such as we hear about with some movie stars. Jesus isn't interested in starting a fan club for himself out of some psychological need for admirers. He craves our love because he wants to fill us with himself. He wants to give us a joy that we can only know by loving him. So as tough as this is to understand, Jesus' thirst for love is a thirst *to give love,* and a thirst to be united with us forever, in the Father's joy. That's why in the meeting with the

Why can't God give us this joy without our consent to his desire and obedience to his will?

Samaritan woman at the well, his *request* for a drink quickly transforms into a *promise* of living water. "Those who drink of the water that I will give them will never be thirsty. The water that I will give will become in them a spring of water gushing up to eternal life" (Jn 4:14).

What does all this mean for us? How can we possibly imitate this? Perhaps the most basic way to imitate the heart of Christ in this dimension is by making our thirst like his. We all hunger and thirst for many things: security, friendship, pleasure, possessions, romance, and so many other needs and wants. Yet this doesn't seem to describe Jesus' thirst. He thirsted above all for souls. He wanted his sacrifice to be worth something. He wanted to save people from their sins and to give them heaven. He thirsted for their conversion so that he could shower them with his gifts. Is this what our thirst looks like? Do we thirst for the salvation of souls? Is our desire for the evangelization of the world so vehement that we can describe it as a *thirst?*

Our response to Christ's thirst isn't exhausted here. We can also *quench* his thirst. Much of the traditional devotion to the Sacred Heart focused on consoling the heart of Christ, making reparation for sins and responding to his love in a more deserving fashion. This desire to repay love for love and to make satisfaction for our own sins and those of others is not outmoded. It is a practical way to quench the very real thirst of Christ's heart. When we teach souls about his love, bring them closer to him through our prayer and good example, and when we ourselves draw nearer to his heart—all these things console him.

Lord, when I see you on the cross, crying out that you thirst, I want to do something. I want to find a way to alleviate your thirst. I know that it wasn't just water that you were longing for—you thirst for me. You thirst for sinners. You thirst for the love of all those you came to save.

Thank you for wanting my love. It would be so hard for me if I thought that my love didn't matter to you. But I know it does. You made yourself needy so that I could satisfy you. You made yourself vulnerable so that I could love you and console you. And if you want it so desperately, my poor love must be worth something. I must be worth something.

Let me find some way today to quench your thirst. Send your Holy Spirit to inspire me during this day so that I will spot real opportunities to show you my love for you and console your heart. Maybe by making some small sacrifice to prove my preference for you above all things. Maybe an act of kindness toward a person in need, knowing that you identify with each one. As you quench my thirst, help me to quench yours.

———◆◆◆◆———

Heart of Jesus, thirsty for the salvation of souls, make my heart more like yours!

June 3

An **undivided** HEART

"You cannot serve two masters."

Lk 16:13

In Jesus' teaching, many times what seem to be commands are really just statements of fact. For instance, Jesus says that he who loves his life will lose it. He says that in order to bear fruit, a grain of wheat needs to fall to the earth and die. Even though he obviously intends a lesson for us, he is not issuing imperatives, but merely telling us about life. Something similar happens when Jesus tells us that "you cannot serve two masters" (Lk 16:13). He isn't so much saying that we *mustn't* serve two masters but rather that it is impossible to do so, so we shouldn't even try. "Don't fool your-

In what circumstances or situations do I tend to vacillate, to hem and haw when I should be firm?

selves," he seems to be saying, "you need to make a choice."

As usual, Jesus perfectly practices what he preaches.

If anyone in history had an undivided heart, it was Jesus. And to what or to whom was this undivided heart devoted? To his Father. There is no wavering, no hemming and hawing, no second guessing. As St. Paul would write years later, "For the Son of God, Jesus Christ… was not 'yes and no'; but in him it is always 'yes'" (2 Cor 1:19). Jesus had no secret vices, no attachments, no crutches he couldn't live without. He had made his choice and stuck with it. He was happily committed and thoroughly faithful.

Throughout salvation history the Israelites—God's chosen people—had struggled with the sin of idolatry. As soon as some crisis hit or they started getting lazy, they would fall back into the worship of other gods. They would weigh their options and try other paths. Even great kings, such as Solomon, allowed themselves to be seduced into this idolatry, which simply means putting something else in God's place. Jesus himself warns of what some of these rivals for God's worship may be: money, power, prestige, comfort, possessions. Anything that promises security in our lives can compete with God for our allegiance.

Which of the world's idols appear most seductive to me personally?

In Jesus' own life, however, we see none of this. He watched over his heart and made sure that nothing unworthy could ever take his Father's place. He used things, he loved people, but he worshipped his Father alone. For this reason, the Father's will was his supreme rule of conduct. In all things, he wanted to please his Father, and he let nothing else usurp God's place. He invites us to be just as single-hearted in following him. In the strongest of terms, Jesus says: "Whoever comes to me and does not hate father and mother, wife and children, brothers and sisters, yes, and even life itself, cannot be my disciple" (Lk 14:26). Obviously Jesus doesn't want us to literally *hate* our parents and siblings, but he does ask for such a radical love that nothing else can compare with it.

Remember, too, that when asked which commandment was the greatest, Jesus unhesitatingly replied: "You shall love the Lord your God with all your heart" (Mt 22:37). I think we can only imagine what it means to truly love God with *all* our heart. What would it be like if we really loved God with all our heart? Jesus did just that. For him, the Father was everything. All other loves—other people, property, affections, projects, and aspirations—were completely subordinated to his boundless love for God.

This doesn't mean, of course, that he didn't truly *love* Philip and John and Mary Magdalene and Lazarus and his own mother. He did! He loved them deeply. But he loved them in God and with God, rather than in God's place. His loves were ordered, not disordered. This may be a hard concept for us to understand, but if we look closely at Jesus' life, we see that this is what he did.

How hard it is for us to love God with this degree of purity and single-heartedness! Many things are so "important" for us that we easily put them on a scale, opposite of God's will, to see which is heaviest! Even when we succeed in making God our supreme value, the greatest love of our heart, we still feel that he is in competition with many other loves and many other goals.

God wants us to love others, there is no doubt about that. He wants us to love them, serve them, and work for their happiness. He has no wish for married people to stop loving their spouses in order to love only him, or for children to stop loving

When I look at my own heart, where do I find evidence of disorder and division?

their parents for fear that they take his place! He wants us to love our friends, coworkers, family members, and even our enemies, but he wants us to love all of them in him, as he loves them. He doesn't want to be put on the same scale with them, as if he were just another creature. He doesn't want to have to compete for our heart. The amazing thing is, the more our love for God grows, the more our love for our neighbor grows along with it.

Lord Jesus, my heart is filled with many loves. Many of them are good and pure; others are disordered and in need of cleansing. I don't think I really love God "with all my heart," the way you love the Father. Please help me with this. Help me to love truly, love profoundly, love intensely. But let me do it always in the right way, with God alone reigning supreme in my heart. I trust that

the better I can do this, the more my love will grow for all your brothers and sisters.

I don't want a divided heart, Lord. I don't want you to have to compete with other gods in my life. You and only you deserve all my love. You have loved me more than anyone else. You created me, redeemed me, and accompany me with your grace and mercy at every moment of my life. You alone are my Lord and my God, fully worthy of all my love and devotion.

Jesus, undivided of heart,
make my heart more like yours!

JUNE 4

A trusting HEART

"I know you always hear me."
Jn 11:42

It's hard to understand how the union of Jesus' divine and human natures works. No, I take that back. It's not just hard, it's *impossible*. But we know, by faith, that Jesus was *truly* God and, at the same time, *truly* man. In these meditations we are focusing especially on Jesus' human nature. By his words and example, Jesus teaches us a lot about God, but he also teaches us what it means to be really human. And one thing we know for sure is that as a man, Jesus trusted God. This means that even when he didn't see things perfectly clearly, or understand why God was asking something of him, or when he didn't feel God's presence, he trusted him anyway.

How deeply am I convinced that God is always watching over me and paying attention to my every need, desire, and prayer?

We glimpse a brief expression of this when Jesus' dear friend Lazarus dies. Jesus is about to raise Lazarus from the dead, but before he does so he looks up to heaven and prays aloud: "Father, I thank you for hearing me. I know that you always hear me; but because of the crowd here I have said this, that they may believe that you sent me" (Jn 11:41-42 NAB). Jesus doesn't say that he *hopes* God hears him, or that he *thinks* that God *probably* hears him. He says: "I *know* that you always hear me." This is absolute confidence.

When Jesus says that the Father "hears" him, he doesn't just mean that in a literal way—that God is aware of what he is saying. After all, a POW may be aware that his hostile guards "hear" his cries for help, yet they turn a deaf ear. This isn't what Jesus intended. By "hearing" Jesus means that God lends a sympathetic ear, always attentive to his needs and difficulties. Remember what the Letter to the Hebrews will say about this later: "In the days of his flesh, Jesus offered up prayers and supplications, with loud cries and tears, to the one who was able to save him from death, and he was heard because of his reverent submission" (Heb 5:7). Here, to say that Jesus was "heard" means that he was answered!

For Jesus, to say that "I know you always hear me" was equivalent to saying, "I know you are always with me. I know you always care for me. I know you always love me. I

Have I ever experienced this "sovereign liberty"? How would my daily life change if I experienced it more deeply and regularly?

know that everything I'm going through matters to you." And we can see throughout his life how this absolute trust in the Father's love made Jesus free and confident. Nothing seemed too big or tough for him because he always had the Father's love. He wasn't afraid of the scribes and Pharisees. He wasn't afraid of the Roman procurator. He wasn't afraid of anything, really, not even suffering and death. His trust in God gave him a sovereign liberty to do whatever he had to do without fearing the consequences.

Jesus' trusting heart was also the key to his fidelity in moments of trial. It is relatively easy, after all, to trust in God when

In which circumstances of life have I found it hardest to trust in God? Why?

everything is going well in life, but much, much harder when times are tough. Many people follow Christ when it makes them feel good, but abandon him as soon as their faith demands sacrifices or when consolation goes away. Jesus wasn't like this. His trust in God was the same in good times and bad. Even at the most difficult moments in his life, he continued to trust. At the Last Supper, he sadly noted that soon his disciples would be scattered and leave him alone, yet he quickly adds: "Yet I am not alone because the Father is with me" (Jn 16:32). And even on the cross, when Jesus no longer felt his Father's presence (indeed, he felt abandoned!), his trust endured: "Father, into your hands I commend my spirit" (Lk 23:46).

This absolute trust wasn't something that Christ intended just for himself because of the special Father-Son relationship he had with God. He intended it for us as well. He assures his disciples that God cares for all his creation, even the birds of the air and the lilies of the field (see Mt 6:26-30). He says that even little sparrows—which are practically worthless—are never forgotten in God's sight, and we are worth far more than they are to God (see Lk 12:6-7). All of this is to help us have the same trust in God that he had.

Lord, I praise you for your trust in the Father! How wonderful to be able to look at you and see what true trust looks like, and to know that it is possible. Glory to you!

In my own life, I often fail at this, and I am sorry for that. Please forgive me. I don't know how many times you have proven your undying love for me, yet in moments of difficulty, I easily begin to doubt again. I don't mean to put you to the test, and I really intend to do better at this. I want to believe in you with unshakeable faith, and to trust in you with rock-solid hope. You are, after all, the only one whom I can truly, totally trust. You will never let me down.

I need a heart more like yours, a heart so confident that I can wake up in the morning and go about my activities with the assurance that you are with me every step of the way: supporting me, encour-

aging me, strengthening me, attentive to my every need. I, too, know that you always hear me. I know that you share my sorrows and my joys. I know that you answer all my prayers, even when I don't immediately get what I wanted or expected.

Heart of Jesus, full of boundless trust in the Father, make my heart more like yours!

JUNE 5

A COMPASSIONATE HEART

"I have compassion for the crowd."
Mk 8:2

All of us have moments when we have had enough. When the in-laws have overstayed their welcome, or the kids

In general, what combination of circumstances tends to bring me to the end of my rope?

have gone beyond the limit, or the job has become so stressful that we can't wait for the clock to strike five, we need some down time. We just want to be left alone to recharge our batteries. We love our fellow man, of course, but enough is enough!

At the end of the day, when we are tired of taking care of others' needs, we would like everyone to just go home.

If a stranger followed me around for two typical days of my life, would they conclude from observing my actions that I have a compassionate heart? Why or why not?

Being human like us, Jesus must have experienced the same thing. From time to time he must have reached the end of his rope. His nerves must have gotten frazzled and he must have longed for some R & R. Yet, even though he must have felt the same frustration, fatigue, and exhaustion that we do, he didn't seem to put any limits on his generosity.

To be sure, Jesus found comfort and strength in his prayer life. Every day, he spent a good bit of time alone with his Father in heartfelt conversation, and these were surely some of his favorite moments of the day. But when people were in need, Jesus never went off duty. He didn't work as a nine-to-five savior, closing up shop and telling people to please come back during working hours. And the reason for this? He had a truly *compassionate* heart. He cared deeply about people and did everything in his power to assist them, despite the sacrifice that required. When another person was suffering or in need, Jesus was there.

We find an emblematic example of this in St. Mark's Gospel. A large crowd had been following Jesus for three days and had nothing to eat. The disciples were all for sending the people home, but Jesus wouldn't hear of it. He says, "I have compassion for the crowd, because they have been with me now for three days and have nothing to eat. If I send them away hungry to their homes, they will faint on the way—and some of them have come from a great distance" (Mk 8:2-3). You remember how the story ends: Jesus multiplies loaves and fishes and feeds them. He sees a need, and he does something about it.

Another day, after hearing that John the Baptist had been killed, Jesus tries to get away in a boat to pray for a while. But the crowds follow him on foot so that when he gets to shore, they are already waiting for him. What is Jesus' response? He doesn't tell them to give him a break. He doesn't slip away. He doesn't get upset. Rather the Gospel says that "he had compassion for them and cured their sick" (Mt 14:12). Jesus truly felt other people's pain. Their sorrows were his sorrows. This

When I think of the word "compassion" does it have positive or negative connotations in my imagination? Why?

is what "compassion" means— the ability to share others' suffering. But his compassion was also "active." He felt pity for others, but he also worked to alleviate it.

St. Paul would later write that the community of believers—the Church—is modeled after the human body. "If one member suffers," he writes, "all suffer together with it; if one member is honored, all rejoice together with it" (1 Cor 12:26). As head of the Church, Jesus gives us the perfect example of this. He was never indifferent to the situation of others. He empathized with others and shared in their lot as if it were his own. Even more so, he puts others' needs *ahead* of his own.

In his first encyclical, Pope Benedict XVI addressed the topic of Christian love. He noted that in her charitable outreach, the Church needs more that "professional competence." He writes: "We are dealing with human beings, and human beings always need something more than technically proper care. They need humanity. They need heartfelt concern" (no. 31.a). Loving others as Christ loved them goes beyond mere philanthropy; it needs a heart like Christ's, which, as Pope Benedict observes, requires "formation of the heart." And he summarized the Christian's program as "'a heart which sees.' This heart sees where love is needed and acts accordingly" (DCE, no. 31b).

How the world would change if all Christians had such a heart! So many problems continue unchecked because our hearts don't see! We might

Who do I know personally that best exemplifies this characteristic of having a "heart that sees"?

have good programs, technically correct solutions, but often what is missing is more compassion. Why is this so difficult for us? Probably for different reasons. Sometimes it's just our selfishness that prevents us from seeing others' troubles, or that keeps us from caring enough to do anything. Sometimes it is our preoccupation with our own projects and concerns. We can be so engrossed in ourselves that others seem to be outside the range of our radar. Other times perhaps we become hardened to others' difficulties— thinking that no one has given us a break, why should we have to solve other people's problems? And so on.

———◦•◦•◦———

Here maybe a good examination of conscience is in order. Is my heart really the way Christ wants it to be? Do I react to others' pain the way Christ did? Am I so wrapped up in my own concerns that I am almost oblivious to the needs of others? If we allow Christ to teach us, we may be surprised at what he tells us. An open heart is the beginning to a Christlike heart.

Lord, thank you for your example of compassion. My own heart easily gravitates to myself and my own interests. I do care about others, but only up to a certain point, and I miss a lot because my heart doesn't always "see" the ways yours does. You weren't indifferent to anyone. Every single human being was important and even precious to you. Let me start today to see people the way you saw them, as dear brothers and sisters entrusted to my care.

I realize, Lord, that to do this I need to think less of myself. I also need to be willing to go beyond my comfort zone. I hate to admit this (but you know it already): many times when I see a person in need, I secretly hope that someone else will do something so that I won't have to. So many times I just don't want to be bothered with others' concerns. That needs to change. If I am truly to have a heart like yours, it must become more selfless and more compassionate.

———◆◇◆———

Heart of Jesus, full of compassion for those around you,
make my heart more like yours!

june 6

A **passionate** HEART

*"Zeal for your house
consumes me."*
Jn 2:17

Some paintings of Jesus make him look so dreamy-eyed and
rosy-cheeked that we could wonder whether he walked with
his feet on the ground or ever got excited about anything.
He comes across more like a 1960s flower child than a
Messiah. It's pretty hard to aspire to that sort of ideal, not
just because it's *unrealistic*, but also because it's *unattractive*.
But I don't think that those paintings do justice to the real
Jesus. Reading through the Gospel accounts we meet a Jesus

When I think of Jesus, what image pops up in my imagination? Why?

with a much richer personality, with great depth, sensitivity, wisdom, and passion.

Remember that the same Jesus who encouraged us to be innocent as doves also invited us to be clever as serpents (see Mt 10:16). The same Jesus who said "Blessed are the meek" (Mt 5:5) also coldly censured the Pharisees, calling them a "brood of vipers" (Mt 12:34) and "whitewashed tombs" (Mt 23:27). It was the same Jesus who embraced little children and cured lepers who also flipped over tables in the temple, making a whip out of cords and driving out animals and money changers (see Jn 2:13-17). It was this last scene that made Jesus' disciples apply to Jesus the Scriptural phrase "Zeal for your house consumes me" (Jn 2:17).

We have already noted that Jesus was no wimp. In fact, he was quite the contrary: he was *passionate*. He was passionate about his mission. He was passionate about the salvation of souls. He was passionate about the Father's glory. He was passionate about redeeming sinners and freeing the downtrodden. He was really passionate about everything he did. Jesus is the opposite of the apathetic, dispassionate, androgynous image we sometimes see on holy cards and devotional posters. Jesus was *on fire* with love for his Father and for souls, and this fire inflamed all his undertakings.

The image of Jesus' heart revealed to St. Margaret Mary Alacoque was surrounded by flames, literally burning with love for

What am I passionate about, if anything? How passionate am I about my friendship with Christ?

us. Something impossible for us to fathom is the depth of Jesus' ardent love for souls. He doesn't just *put up* with us. He doesn't just *bear* with us. He doesn't even just *like* us. His heart is consumed with love for us. Think about the time you were most in love, multiply it by infinity, and you get a sense of how Jesus feels about us. And "us" here doesn't mean the mass of humanity. It means YOU. Jesus is literally dying for you to be in heaven with him. Not only you, of course. Walk down the street or through a shopping mall sometime and look around at the people. Consider that each one of them (some of whom you would never notice) is loved by Jesus in this passionate way. Each one is important. Each one occupies the heart of Jesus in a unique, singular way.

How deeply do I believe that God created me to be a saint, to be a passionate follower of Jesus Christ?

We Christians are called to be passionate like Christ. Our hearts should burn with love for God, for Jesus, for Mary, for the Church, and for our brothers and sisters. Christianity is not a religion of quiet tea parties and platonic goodwill towards all. It is a religion of martyrs and confessors, of men and women who believe that their faith in Jesus Christ is worth living and dying for. It is said that our generation is infected with a subtle nihilism where nothing really matters too much. Fortunately, there are still many who believe enough to follow Jesus in a radical way and who love him with true passion.

———◆◆◆———

That doesn't mean that Christians should be running around like a bunch of crazed fanatics, jumping up on soapboxes and screaming about the end of the world. Not much is accomplished for Christ's kingdom by acting like religious lunatics. Look again to Jesus. He was passionate, yes, and his passion motivated his work and gave him energy for the mission. Yet Jesus united his passion to his reason, order-ing his behavior according to the Father's will. If you will excuse the analogy, it's not enough for a race car to have a powerful engine; it also needs brakes and a steering wheel! So Jesus was both active and serene, both passionate and peaceful—yet never complacent or inert. His love expressed itself in many different ways, but it was always the same love underneath.

Thank you, my Jesus, for loving me with such passion! Thank you for calling me into existence and for choosing me to be your disciple, granting me the priceless gift of faith in you! Thank you for looking on me with love, despite my unworthiness! Who am I, after all, that you should love me so much? Who am I that you should pursue me with such ardor? Who am I that you should die for me on the cross? And yet you do and you have!

I am amazed when I consider that there is nothing you wouldn't do for me. It seems that your whole life was a poem of passionate love for me. The only way I can repay you is to love you in the same way.

Lord, as I draw near to your Sacred Heart, a bonfire of love for the Father and for souls, let me be ignited with the fire of your love. Shake me out of my apathy and laziness, so I can be a true apostle of your Kingdom. Let me experience your love more deeply every day, so that I am moved to love you passionately in return. Let me burn with your fire, love with your love, and feel what you feel toward all those around me!

━━━◆◆◆◆━━━

Jesus, passionate of heart,
make my heart more like yours!

JUNE 7

A **personal** HEART

*"I know my own
and my own know me."*
Jn 10:14

The *Peanuts* character Linus once quipped, "I love mankind; it's *people* I can't stand." This sentiment could be applied to many of us. It's much easier to love *humanity* than it is to love the greasy guy sitting next to you on the bus, or the driver who cuts you off on the road. It's easier to love faraway folks and entire classes of people ("the poor," "the starving in Ethiopia," "the unemployed") than it is to love the real flesh and blood you run into every day. Mankind as a group is one

A HEART LIKE HIS

thing, but when we get down to the nuts and bolts of real human beings with all their quirks and foibles, love becomes far more demanding.

We sometimes misapply this vice to God himself. We know that he loves "mankind." We know that he so loved "the world" that he sent his only Son as savior. Yet we can't really believe that he loves grumpy Mr. Fisk or smelly Mrs. French. Sometimes we can't even believe he loves us. So open your Gospel again and look at Jesus. What do you discover? You discover a good shepherd, who knows every sheep by name. You find a shepherd for whom every single individual sheep is so important that he would leave ninety-nine sheep in the wilderness to seek out one that strayed. You don't meet a Messiah of numbers or of percentages but a Messiah for whom every one counts.

This is very impressive. We are used to a utilitarian ethic, whereby we look for the greatest happiness of the greatest number, despite the unhappy consequence that some will fall through the cracks. As long as *most* people are okay,

Who do I tend to consider "important" and who do I tend to consider "not important"?

we figure we're doing pretty well. That wasn't Jesus' ethics at all. All it took was *one* person in need to move Jesus' heart. All it took was a *single* individual (even an unworthy, sinful individual) to set him in action. For Jesus, human beings were never numbers; they were always persons. And for Jesus, every person was irreplaceable. He didn't distinguish between important people and unimportant people. All were of infinite worth to him.

That's why Jesus makes time for everyone. That's why Jesus treats each person with the same respect. Jesus never made "quality of life" judgments to see who deserved his attention and his care. For him, every human life had the essential quality of being his brother and sister. That was enough.

The Gospels often speak of Jesus addressing the "crowds" that followed after him, yet time after time they also narrate his encounters with real-life people: widows, soldiers, prostitutes, paralytics, lepers, beggars, and so on. They tell us of Jesus' meeting with Jairus the synagogue official and Zacchaeus the tax collector and Simon the leper and of course, Mary Magdalene "from whom seven demons had gone out." Day after day,

Jesus devoted himself to real people, with names, addresses, personal histories, and individual needs.

———◆◆◆◆◆———

Why do I tend to be more patient towards my own failings than towards the flaws and foibles of others?

Sometimes, too, we can romanticize what these people were like to deal with on a daily basis. Jesus didn't love them because they were such fine people that one couldn't help but love them. Most of the people Jesus dealt with were petty, short-sighted, and deeply flawed. Some were cheats. Others were scheming. Still others were lazy, lustful, and dishonest. Yet Jesus *loved* those people, the imperfect and often unpleasant ones.

To have a heart like Christ's means to have a heart that sees every human being as precious. It means a personal touch in our dealings with others, even if they are "only" the check-out clerk at the grocery store or the shampoo girl at the hair salon. Loving humanity must translate into loving the person next to me right now. The maxim "charity begins at home" has special significance in this context. The people we rub shoulders with every day—especially our immediate family—are often those we find it hardest to love, simply because we have to deal with them every day. Yet in those all-too-real people beside us, with all their limitations and annoying habits, we discover our special vocation to Christian charity.

I bless you, Lord, for your example of personal love. You didn't set up all sorts of programs and associations for charitable work. You reached out personally and touched people, one by one. You looked at them, knew them, and loved them. You went out in search of the lost, in order to bring them home. You looked deep into people's hearts, beyond their obvious failings, to discover a hidden beauty, the image of God in all of them. Your love for them made them beautiful in your eyes. Thank you!

I too easily fall into the habit of ignoring those closest to me. I am moved with pity when I hear of people suffering from natural disasters far away or when I read of tragic situations. At the same time, I am often closed to those nearest to me, especially when I don't feel natural affection for them or when they get on my nerves. I am sorry for this. Please forgive me.

Teach me to see each person through your eyes and with your heart. Help me to look beyond their defects and to see the beauty of your image in all of them. Let me love them one by one, without excluding anyone. Help me discover what they need and what I can do for them. I want to start today.

———— ❈ ————

Heart of Jesus, imbued with personal love,
make my heart more like yours!

June 8

A pious HEART

"Ask and you will receive."
Lk 11:9

God isn't a genie in a bottle. We sometimes resist asking God for favors because we unconsciously think we need to "save" our requests for something more important, as if God were a genie who only grants three wishes. So instead of "bothering" God over our little needs and aspirations, we sometimes wait until Grandma is sick or some other really important crisis occurs to "use up" our petitions. Somehow, we think that this way, we are more likely to be answered. No sense in using up our quota ahead of time!

If I were more aware of God's constant attention to me and my needs, how would it affect my daily life?

We smile at this description because none of us consciously acts this way, although all of us recognize ourselves at least a little in it. Now let's turn to Jesus.

What was his attitude toward divine requests? We all know that he encouraged his followers to ask for things from God. He tells us to ask, to seek, and to knock, and he promises that we will be heard and answered. He spurs us to boldness of faith, believing that we have already received what we are asking for (see Mk 11:24)! And if God should seem to tarry in responding, Jesus recommends that we "wear God out" by asking over and over until we get satisfaction (Lk 18:1-8)!

At the same time, Jesus also reminds us that God "knows what you need before you ask him" (Mt 6:8), so we don't have to be exhaustive in our requests for fear of forgetting something and God never finding out! We're not "informing" God about our needs and desires; we are expressing them and asking his intervention.

In his own life, Jesus practiced all these counsels. He exhibited an endearing familiarity with God together with deep respect.

In the ancient Roman world, this childlike virtue was called *piety*. It was the virtue that good sons or daughters

When I address God as "Father," what sentiments rise up in my heart? Why?

should have in relation with their parents. Unlike our modern notions of piety, which are more limited to religious devotion, the classical virtue referred to our natural parents as well. Jesus called God "Father," or even *Abba* ("Dad"). He conversed with him easily and often, and put all his needs and cares in his hands. For Jesus, God wasn't some magical genie who grants wishes but a loving Father who is closely attentive to the needs of his children.

We can sometimes think that petition is the least noble form of prayer. We know that our relationship with God should go beyond the fulfillment of our requests. We know that we often neglect other important forms of prayer—such as praise, adoration, contrition, and thanksgiving—and focus predominantly on petition. But this doesn't mean there is anything wrong or contemptible with asking God for everything we need. We are, after all, poor, weak creatures with a daily need for God's gifts. We depend on him, and our frequent requests remind us of this dependence. Remember that the Our Father—the prayer Jesus taught his disciples—contains no less that seven petitions! In the end, we are God's beloved children, for whom he is happy to provide.

Do I tend to evaluate God's fatherhood in terms of my experience with my own human parents, or vice versa?

Years ago, my mother told me that whenever she had to travel by plane, she asked Jesus for good weather because she was frightened. She said that her prayer was always answered. You can dismiss this as silly superstition or a misuse of prayer, but I have always thought that such childlike simplicity was beautiful. The more aware we are of God's fatherly love for us, the more convinced we will be that he wills all good things for us. A mother's or father's care isn't limited to the "big things" like giving birth or paying college tuition but reaches to the little details of every day (making dinner, having time to listen to our problems, helping us fix the car, etc.). Is God's love for us any less attentive?

Jesus prayed all the time. He prayed in public and in private, in the synagogue and in the temple, in the desert and in the mountains, aloud and silently. We find him praising God and thanking him, but we also find him asking God for what he needs, most poignantly in the Garden of Gethsemani, where he begs his Father to let this cup pass him by (see Lk 22:42). He reveals to us a God who *wants* to be asked, a Father who *delights* in seeing us approach him confidently with our requests. Again, it's not because God doesn't already know what we need; he just likes to hear it coming from us.

Lord, what a beautiful example you give me of confident, pious love for your Father! You trusted in him for all your needs, and confided to him all your secrets. He was not only your Father but also your provider and best friend. You were happy to be God's son and to depend on him for everything. This didn't make you feel smaller or less free but happier and more secure. Blessed be your holy name!

As you know, I do make lots of requests to God. I think, however, that I need to do so with greater faith and confidence in his love. I also need to do so with more childlike simplicity and trust. Grant me a truly "pious" heart like yours, the heart of a son. I'm not an employee asking for favors from his boss or a citizen asking for an audience with the local government official. I am a beloved son, who appeals to his father for all his needs, sure of getting a hearing!

It helps me, Lord, to remember that God wants me to ask. He delights in my requests and in being able to come to my assistance when I call to him. I'm not a burden to him but a joy. Let me always praise and thank you (I don't do this enough!), but let me also make many requests, even for simple things. Let me desire your greatest gifts above all, especially my own sanctification and the salvation of souls, but don't let this stop me from placing even my smallest cares into God's hands.

Pious heart of Jesus, true son of the Father,
make my heart more like yours!

JUNE 9

A **pure** HEART

"Blessed are the pure in heart."
Mt 5:8

Pope John Paul II once wrote that the Beatitudes are Jesus'
"self-portrait."[1] In a series of brief vignettes, Jesus describes
the blessed life and the basic attitudes and dispositions
that underlie true holiness. In so doing, however, Jesus also
describes himself. He, more perfectly than anyone else, is
"poor in spirit," "merciful," "meek," a "peacemaker." And he
is also perfectly "pure in heart."

---

1   Pope John Paul II, encyclical letter, *Veritatis Splendor* (1993), no. 16.

By emphasizing purity of heart, Jesus isn't taking away from the importance of being pure in mind and body as well, but he underscores the heart once again as the center of our being. It is above all our *love* that must be pure—untainted by anything unworthy.

What is purity, after all, if not the absence of foreign elements that would corrupt or diminish the authenticity of something? Pure, twenty-four-karat gold contains no such foreign elements. It is unmingled, unalloyed, and unadulterated. What you see is what you get. The same can be said for pure single-malt Scotch whiskey, pure maple syrup, or pure cashmere. They are all one hundred percent what they claim to be.

When I think of the phrase "pure in heart," what pops into my imagination? Why?

Purity means authenticity. It has nothing to do with prudery or Puritanism or hatred of the human body. And this authenticity is what we see throughout Jesus' life. He was not pure in heart just because he was celibate. His heart was pure because he loved truly, without self-interest or second intentions. He looked on others not as objects from whom he could derive some gain, but as persons. He didn't *desire* people to please himself but *loved* them for their own sake. And that is why Jesus' gaze didn't bring shame or embarrassment but a sense of security and peace.

Look at the way that Jesus treats the woman known as a "sinner" in the town (see Lk 7:36-50). You will recall that Jesus was at the home of

Why do you think that the spirit of lust is always associated with terms like "dirty" and "filthy"?

Simon the Pharisee when this woman comes in and sits at Jesus' feet. She weeps over his feet and dries them with her hair. Then she kisses his feet and anoints them with ointment. Simon is appalled at this and thinks to himself that Jesus couldn't be a prophet; otherwise, he would know what kind of a woman was touching him—a sinner.

Yet, what was going on in this woman's heart? How did she experience Jesus? Usually, when women were referred to as "sinners" in the ancient world, the label referred to adulteresses and prostitutes. This woman surely knew what it was to be "used" by men. She could easily distinguish between a sensual leer and a gaze of love. In Jesus, she found acceptance for who she was as a person. She found love and forgiveness rather than self-interest and lust, and she poured out love in return—so much so that Jesus said to Simon that it was precisely because she had experienced God's mercy that she showed such great love.

Jesus loved his Father with a pure heart—free from pettiness and mixed intentions. He loved men and women, boys and girls with this same purity. His love was simple and untainted, clean and unblemished. He didn't allow anything to stain his love.

When we speak of purity, we often compare it to "the driven snow" or "mountain spring water." We are suspicious of "additives" and are starting to request "no preservatives," "no artificial coloring," "no artificial sweeteners," "no hormones," "no caffeine," "no MSG," and so on. This was Jesus, the savior with no artificial anything. Jesus, pure and simple. Little children felt attracted to him. Men and women felt attracted to him. He wasn't opportunistic or threatening. He just was there for them, no strings attached.

———◆◆◆◆◆———

This is the sort of purity of heart to which we are called. It isn't easy, because self-interest always seems to worm its way into our relationships, despite our best efforts to keep it out. Even if our primary motive is good, we often discover secondary motives for our actions that are not so noble. Relationships that can start out pure can become corrupted over time. This is surely why Jesus recommends that we both pray and "watch." The human heart requires constant purification. The Bible compares this purification to the refining of precious metals and the bleaching of white garments. These processes can be painful. To refine gold it must be heated to a high temperature so that the dross will float to the top, to be skimmed off. To bleach garments, a fuller would use lye—a highly concentrated form of potassium hydroxide that burned away stains. Examining our conscience helps us to unearth the impurities that can stain our love. But we also need the purifying power of God's grace, the fire of his love.

Lord, I so admire the purity of your Sacred Heart. You were able to love so intensely, so passionately, and yet so purely. You weren't out for personal gain or to see what was in it for you. You loved others for their sake. Blessed be your holy name!

I love, too, Lord; you know I do. But you also know how desperately I need you to purify my love. I want a clean heart like yours, a heart cleansed of pettiness, lusts, clinginess, greed, its envy of others, grudges, complexes, and bitterness. Grant me a pure heart, a free heart, a heart filled with love for God and for my neighbor. Let me love purely, which is to love truly and authentically.

I pray for our society, too, Lord. Help us to rediscover the beauty of purity. Help us to appreciate it as a gift to be treasured and preserved, not sold and traded. All the connected virtues, too, dear Jesus—modesty, chastity, humility, and simplicity—renew our love for these virtues that we need so much.

⚬⚬⚬

Jesus, pure and clean of heart,
make my heart more like yours!

A **merciful** HEART

*"Today you will be with me
in paradise."*
Mt 9:13

As little children, we are taught that God is infinitely merciful and infinitely just. It is a mystery, we are told, how these two qualities coincide in God. It would seem that they are in opposition, and that one must eventually predominate. Justice, after all, means that people get what is coming to them, right? And mercy means that we don't get what's coming to us! So which is it?

Is my natural tendency more towards treating others with harsh justice or with patient mercy?

In the Gospel, Jesus does indeed talk about both judgment and mercy. He assures us that there will be a final reckoning, and we will have to give an accounting for our actions. On the other hand, he also assures us that mercy is available even for the worst sinners, and that he came to take away our sins, rather than condemn us for them. In the Cross, justice and mercy kiss because Jesus takes justice upon himself, receiving what we deserve and giving us what we do not deserve. And so the prophet Isaiah's words are fulfilled: "Through his stripes we are healed" (Is 53:5). In the end, love triumphs, and it does so under the form of mercy.

The heart of Jesus is a heart rich in mercy, a heart that is moved with pity in the face of human misery, especially the moral misery of sin. Jesus is not an uninterested judge, dispensing rewards and punishments with the same indifference. Like the Father, Jesus does not desire the death of the sinner, but that he turn from his evil ways and live (see Ezek 18:23). When the paralytic is presented before him, Jesus responds by giving the greatest gift he has. Rather than cure his physical malady, Jesus offers a more magnificent prize: "Son, your sins are forgiven" (Mk 2:5). He defends his constant company-keeping with sinners by reminding his hearers that he is a physician, who has come not for the healthy but for the sick (see Mt 9:11-13). His entire mission, in fact, is a mission of mercy![1] He comes among us as a man to free us from sin and win our redemption. Pope John Paul did not hesitate to say that Jesus' words, "Blessed are the merciful," constitute "a synthesis of the whole of the Good News"![2]

Why is God so merciful?

Perhaps the most touching example of this came at the end of Jesus' life, as he hung between heaven and earth on the cross, with his blood and breath slowly leaving his body. We don't know why, but one of the two thieves crucified with Jesus turns to the other thief to rebuke him. He recognizes that both of them are getting their just deserts, whereas Jesus has done nothing wrong. He then turns to Jesus and utters the most important words of his entire life: "Jesus, remember me

---

1 Pope John Paul II would write in striking language that "mercy constitutes the fundamental content of the messianic message of Christ and the constitutive power of His mission" (Pope John Paul II, encyclical letter, *Dives in Misericordia* [1980], no. 6).

2 Pope John Paul II, encyclical letter *Dives in Misericordia* (1980), no. 8.

when you come into your kingdom" (Lk 23:42). Who knows what he expected to hear, but it couldn't have been as marvellous as the response he received. Without hesitating, Jesus turned to him and simply said: "Truly I tell you, today you will be with me in paradise" (Lk 23:43).

Why does popular culture tend to give more attention to vengeance than forgiveness?

Why is it that we do not feel the same pity for sinners that Jesus felt? Why are we moved at the suffering of a beaver with its leg caught in a trap, and yet feel nothing but anger and disdain for sinners? Perhaps we feel that they had a choice, that it is their own fault. They made their own bed—we reason—and now they must lie in it. Our choices have consequences, and they chose badly. Yet I fear that when we reason in this way we separate ourselves radically from the heart of Christ. The pagans revered justice as the greatest virtue, but mercy distinguishes the Christian.

In a real sense, when we are merciful we touch the most characteristic quality of Christ's own heart. We resemble him in the most intimate way possible. As Pope John Paul wrote, during the time of our earthly existence, "Love must be revealed above all as mercy and must also be actualized as mercy."[3] If we want to know whether we love like Christ, we must ask ourselves whether our heart is merciful as his was. Without mercy, love is impossible.

When, perhaps rightly, we feel indignation and even anger toward sinners who hurt others and disturb the social order, before we consign them to hell we should ask ourselves: "Would I be willing to die for him? Do I, like Christ, find no pleasure in his punishment but desire above all his conversion?" And we should realistically consider where we would be without that mercy. Would you really like to be judged simply on your own merits? I wouldn't. All of us have desperate need of God's mercy, whether we realize it or not.

As John Paul once noted: "The present-day mentality, more perhaps than that of people in the past, seems opposed to a God of mercy."[4] We find it weak, unrealistic, intolerable,

3   Pope John Paul II, encyclical letter *Dives in misericordia* (1980), no. 8.
4   Pope John Paul II, encyclical letter *Dives in misericordia* (1980), no. 2.

and even socially destructive. And yet Jesus said, "I desire mercy, not sacrifice" (Mt 9:13). We must hate sin—in our own lives and others'—yet even more so we must love sinners, as Christ did. Otherwise, we will have no part with him.

Lord, what can I say? Where would I be without your infinite mercy? How many times have I turned to you in sorrow only to hear those saving words: "My child, I forgive you"? Let me always have your mercy before my eyes, so that I will not be tempted to desire for others a punishment that I have been spared.

Sin is a terrible thing. It rends the social fabric. It breaks up families. It destroys lives. Help me to detest sin and do what I can to eradicate it, above all in my own life. At the same time, let me look on my fellow sinners with a heart of mercy, with your own heart. If I am to err, Lord, let it be on the side of mercy. Let me prefer to be too indulgent, rather than even once to be too severe in my judgments.

When I look on your life, I am moved by your merciful love. You felt the effects of sin in your own flesh, and yet you are the first to excuse, to pardon, to welcome back into your friendship. Praised be your gentle, merciful heart! Praised be your revelation of a Father who is rich in mercy!

———◆◆◆———

Heart of Jesus, bursting with merciful love,
make my heart more like yours!

JUNE 11

AN **honest** HEART

*"Out of the abundance of the heart,
the mouth speaks."*

Mt 12:34

No one likes to get "played." We like people to be straight with us, to tell us the truth, and to call a spade a spade. Jesus felt the same abhorrence for dishonesty, hypocrisy, and duplicity and called people on these vices over and over. He himself was quite the opposite. He was always truthful. More than that, he was "the truth" (Jn 14:6).

Jesus called the devil "the father of lies" (Jn 8:44). When he lies, Jesus said, "he speaks according to his own nature" because "there is no truth in him" (Jn 8:44). A liar's heart brings forth lies. Jesus, on the other hand, draws truth from a heart committed to the truth. "For this I was born, and for this I came into the world, to testify to the truth. Everyone who belongs to the truth listens to my voice" (Jn 18:13).

Why, at times, is lying such a powerful temptation for us?

Jesus didn't invent fables to get us to behave. He tells only the truth. Even his parables reveal only the truth. He tells the truth about God, about judgment, about human nature, about heaven and hell, about the meaning of life. We can trust him because no matter what the consequences, he never lied. "Which of you convicts me of sin? If I tell the truth, why do you not believe me?" (Jn 8:46). There is something deeply comforting about a person who will always tell you the truth. Jesus is like that. We can count on him always to tell us the truth, whether it be tough or easy for us to hear. And yet he also does so with love: *caritas in veritate*.

Jesus assures us that this truth will "set us free" (Jn 8:32). It sets us free, in the first place, because it liberates us from error and false notions about God and ourselves. Ignorance is always a sort of slavery, especially when we are illiterate about the things that matter most. It's not too important when we are ignorant about astrophysics

What does popular culture usually try to tell us about the relationship between truth and freedom?

or molecular biology, but it's terrible when we are misinformed regarding the meaning of life, where we come from, and where we are going. But the truth also sets us free because the person who lives in the truth lives in light, both inside and outside. He is transparent and authentic. Duplicity slowly corrodes and darkens the soul, whereas integrity—living according to the truth—makes a person freer and freer.

There were many times when Jesus would have benefited from a little white lie. His truthfulness got him into lots of trouble, especially with the scribes and Pharisees. When on trial before Pilate or the Sanhedrin, Jesus keeps telling it like it is. He doesn't look for legal loopholes or clever rhetoric to confuse the issue. "Are you a king?" Pilate asks. "Yes, I am," responds Jesus (Jn 18:37). "Are you the Messiah, the son of God?" asks the high priest. "You have said it," replies Jesus, "and you will see the Son of Man seated at the right hand of Power and coming on the clouds of heaven" (Mt 26:64).

How do I tend to act when telling the truth is inconvenient?

Hardly a diplomatic answer. Jesus tells the truth and accepts the consequences.

Jesus lived the deepest integrity known to humanity. He spoke the truth. He lived the truth. There were no divisions in his personality. He didn't have a professional side and a private side—he simply was who he was. And he was the "light of the world," revealing the truth and illuminating our darkness.

———◆◆◆———

We are called to live the same sort of integrity, ordering all our words and actions according to our deepest beliefs. We are called to be a light for others, shining truth where there is only darkness, ignorance, and sin.

Lord Jesus, thank you for always telling me the truth. I am so happy to be able to count on you to tell it like it is. You showed us the Father's face. You revealed to us where we come from and where we are going. You taught us about right and wrong, about

good and evil, about death and judgment, about heaven and hell. We would still be in the dark about so many things, if you hadn't chosen to enlighten us. Thank you!

But thanks even more for your witness of truthfulness and integrity. Not many in this world of ours truly practice what they preach. I have been let down so many times by people I counted on but never by you. May this be a lesson for me to trust only in you! You not only told the truth, you also lived it. Your actions bear witness to the truth of your words. You preached love and you lived love. You preached mercy and you lived mercy. You preached humility and you lived that too. Thank you!

I, too, am called to live in the light. I am called to bear witness to the truth both through my words and through my actions. May the same integrity that filled your heart fill mine as well. Let there be no room in my heart for deceit, duplicity or hypocrisy. Let me always act with the awareness that you see me, you are with me, and everything is visible to your eyes, even my most hidden intentions!

Heart of Jesus, model of honesty and integrity,
make my heart more like yours!

JUNE 12

A *poor* HEART

"Nowhere to lay his head."
Lk 9:58

Poverty is usually an imposition, not a choice. Many people are born poor and live poor all their lives, but few do so willingly. Why after all would someone elect to have less rather than more? Well, that's precisely what Jesus did. St. Paul sums this up neatly: "For you know the generous act of our Lord Jesus Christ, that though he was rich, yet for your sakes he became poor, so that by his poverty you might become rich" (2 Cor 8:9).

Jesus actually chose poverty for himself. He could have been born in a palace, but he chose to be born in a cave.... How deeply have I thought about this choice that Jesus made?

Throughout the centuries, many have interpreted the Christian exaltation of poverty as a rejection of the world. But this isn't it at all. From the beginning, Christians have understood that all creation is good and comes from the hand of God. He made the world and everything in it for us, to show us his love for us and to provide for all our needs. We are not so "spiritual" that we see material creation as evil!

So how can we understand Jesus' choice for poverty and the Christian tradition? St. Teresa of Ávila had a little saying that can shed some light on this. She said, "Whoever has God wants for nothing. God alone suffices." The human heart easily imagines needs for itself. We may feel that there are a million and one things that we cannot do without. These multiplying needs not only can distract us, they also can threaten to take God's place in our lives as the one thing that is truly necessary. Remember Jesus' gentle rebuke of Martha: "Martha, Martha, you are worried and distracted by many things; there is need of only one thing" (Lk 10:41-42).

Jesus didn't choose material poverty for its own sake. He did so because his heart was

To what extent do certain material possessions (or the desire for certain material possessions) "possess my heart"?

poor. It was detached from all the "things" that we humans so readily crave and cling to. Because his heart was poor, Jesus was truly free. The funny thing is, we think that the more we have the freer we will be, but usually the opposite is true. We easily become possessed by what we possess. We serve things, instead of letting them serve us. Jesus never fell into that trap. He kept his heart focused on the Father's love and others' needs, and not on possessions.

At the same time, Jesus never despised material things. He used what he had, without ever setting his heart on it. He came to bring good news to the poor, but he also showed that there are many kinds of poverty. The truly poor person is the one who is far from God because he lacks true riches. So Jesus dealt with rich and poor, educated and illiterate, popular folk and outcasts. He recognized the needs of each one and sought to alleviate them. He didn't offer technical solutions, organize massive fundraising drives, or create philanthropic associations (not that there is anything wrong with these initiatives in themselves). He gave us God. He revealed to us the Father's love. He offered us all "a share in his riches."[1]

Jesus invites his followers to opt for poverty the way he did. Remember that when a scribe approached Jesus and said, "Teacher, I will follow you wherever you go," Jesus didn't answer: "Great, happy to have you on board!" He first wanted to make sure that the man knew what he was in for, and so he said, "Foxes have holes, and birds of the air have nests; but the Son of Man has nowhere to lay his head" (Mt 8:19-20).

If I were more thoroughly convinced that I am only a "pilgrim" in this life, how would my daily living change?

By following Jesus, we also accept his conditions, and one of these is detachment. He reminds us that we are pilgrims passing through, with no lasting city in this world. He wants us to have a poor heart, like

---

1   From the preface for the Eucharistic Prayer, Weekdays I.

his. He invites us to the simplicity of an uncluttered life, and even more important, an uncluttered heart! He doesn't want our hearts complicated with cobwebs, hidden cupboards, dark corners, and cubby holes. Sweep it. Clean it. Let the light of Christ illuminate everything.

Lord Jesus, thank you for your example of poverty. The absence of many things in your life didn't make you glum, it just made you peaceful. You didn't spend your time running around chasing after things. You used your time and your attention for greater things. Because you weren't attached to things, you had more time for prayer and for service. Blessed be your holy name!

My heart isn't as free as yours. If I am honest, I see that I am attached to many things, material and immaterial. I am sure that I care too much about having nice things, what people think of me, and where I will go on vacation. Surely these "harmless" little attachments clutter my heart and disturb my peace of mind.
I know you put me in this world to make a difference, Lord. I have to deal with material realities every day. I have a family budget

and real physical needs, and many people depend on me. Help me to deal with all these things responsibly but without ever setting my heart on them. Keep me poor in the midst of the world, using things but loving only you!

Jesus, poor of heart,
make my heart more like yours!

JUNE 13

A disciplined HEART

"Long before dawn..."
Mt 11:29

Since Jesus was not just a man but also God, we readily assume that things had to be easier for him than they are for us. After all—we think—how tough could it be, if he was really God? In these meditations on the Sacred Heart of Christ, we should remember that his humanity was no act. He didn't just "go through the motions" of being human like us. He really was. The Letter to the Hebrews insists that "we do not have a high priest who is unable to sympathize with our weaknesses, but we have one who in every respect has been tested as we are, yet without sin" (Heb 4:15). In other words, all the aches and pains, all the trials and tribulations of weak humanity, were Jesus' as well. That should give us courage but also challenge us.

Which of my normal responsibilities do I usually feel like doing? Which do I usually not feel like doing?

For example, St. Mark relates how Jesus got up "in the morning, long before dawn" to go off to a lonely place to pray (Mk 1:35). For those of us who sometimes have trouble getting up in the morning, this should give us pause. It's not that Jesus bounced out of bed every day, feeling like a million bucks. Sometimes he woke up tired, sometimes he slept badly on the uneven ground, sometimes he awoke with a headache or backache, and sometimes he surely felt like rolling over and sleeping a few more hours. This meditation isn't about Jesus' sleeping habits, however—it's about his willpower. Jesus had a *disciplined* heart, which often had him doing not what he felt like but what he knew he should.

The prophet Jeremiah expressed misgivings about undisciplined hearts with the following words: "More tortuous than all else is the human heart, beyond remedy; who can understand it?" (Jer 17:9). It's true that many people make bad decisions by "following their heart" rather than their head. Think, for example, of the young woman who marries an irresponsible playboy, because she is "in love,"

What governs my decisions day by day: reason enlightened by faith, or vague, superficial feelings and passing moods?

rather than listening to the warnings of good friends and even her own reason! Yet because Jesus' heart was disciplined, his decisions were not based on flights of fancy or inclinations of the moment but on deeper principles. His heart was well-ordered and governed by reason, rather than at odds with it.

Jesus' grueling schedule, and especially his ever-present awareness that he was to suffer terribly and die for us on a cross, demanded an incredible degree of self-discipline. Each day, when he woke up, he knew he was one day closer to Calvary. Yet it wasn't stoicism that kept him on track; it was the deep love he bore for his Father and for each of us. Love, and not some strange sense of "duty for duty's sake," was the driving force behind Jesus' self-mastery. His was a heart disciplined by love, urged on by love, compelled by love. Love isn't fickle or on-again, off-again. It is constant. So, far from being at odds with discipline, true love requires it.

Why do we—and our society—tend to disassociate discipline and love?

In many places in today's society and popular culture, discipline is out of fashion, since people equate it with intransigence and a lack of spontaneity. In Jesus' case, however, discipline didn't make him less flexible but more. You remember the beautiful parable of the Good Samaritan, where Jesus implicitly criticizes the priest and the Levite for their failure to stop and assist the poor fellow who had fallen in with brigands (see Lk 10:30-37). Both the priest and the Levite were going along the road, no doubt intent on the "good things" they had to do in the next town; yet, the tightness of their "program" kept them from helping the needy person God had put directly in their path. Now, compare this attitude to that of Jesus. Many of his most poignant encounters were "unplanned," and he always seemed to find time for everyone, despite his incredibly full schedule. You may recall that in the case of the woman with the hemorrhage, Jesus cured her while he was on the way to cure someone else—the daughter of Jairus, a leader of the synagogue (see Luke 8:41-56)!

———◈◆◈———

If they are to be constant and successful, our prayer life, family life, and work life demand more than good intentions. They require a disciplined heart. We need to stick with our resolutions and choose the best thing and not just what seems most fun or pleasing

When was the last time I didn't follow through on a good resolution? Why didn't I?

in the moment. How many times we make good proposals or promise all sorts of things to God, only to see ourselves back in the same rut not long afterward? Don't we often suffer from a heart that lacks discipline? Jesus shows us that a truly loving heart is a selfless heart—a disciplined heart.

Lord, I realize that having a heart like your means more than just good intentions. It also means constancy. You know, Lord, that discipline scares me. It just sounds so hard and so unpleasant. Help me to realize that it doesn't have to be like that, if I keep in mind that self-discipline is just another name for true love. Help me love you so much that the little sacrifices required by my fidelity become sweet—like so many chances to show how much I love you. Let my devotion to duty never become dry or heartless, but keep it full of love.

Show me, Jesus, where I need to grow most in this virtue. Where would you like me to practice greater self-discipline? How can my heart be more united to my reason and faith, so that my life is governed by my deepest principles and not just by my feelings? I know that to advance at all in this, I need your grace. I need you to fill my heart with a more profound love for you and for the many people I deal with every day. Give me just a taste of your love, just a splinter, just a spark of the bonfire that is your Heart. That will be enough for me!

❖

Heart of Jesus, disciplined and driven by love,
make my heart more like yours!

JUNE 14

An **unpretentious** HEART

*"Do not let your left hand know
what your right hand is doing."*
Mt 6:3

If you visit fine buildings on college campuses, you will often discover a bronze plaque attesting to the generosity of some benefactor. "This science wing was made possible by a grant from the Wellmore Foundation." "The Teahouse Auditorium was a gift from Mrs. Margaret Esther Teahouse." Human beings can be very, very generous with their time and money. But they also like to be recognized for their donations.

Jesus told his disciples that his new law was tougher than the old law. People sometimes think that he made things easier by summing up all of the commandments into love of God and love of neighbor, but in reality love can be much more demanding than following a list of rules. He said that the old law forbade adultery, but the new law demanded purity of heart, including not even looking at a woman lustfully. He said that whereas the old law forbade murder, the new law prohibited anger with one's brother and even the use of harsh language (see Mt 5:20-28). In the same way, Jesus invited his followers to a great purity of intention and a disinterested heart.

When was the last time I did the right thing for the wrong reason?

Jesus recognized that we often do the right thing for the wrong reason. For instance, sometimes we pray publicly in order to be thought of as holy or pious. Sometimes, people give alms in order to be praised or thought of highly. And Jesus unmasked these practices, because he didn't want our twisted intentions to deprive us of the rewards he has in store for us. His new law was all about having both our inside and our outside in line with God's will. In his own words, he doesn't just want us "good," he wants us *perfect!*

96

AN UNPRETENTIOUS HEART JUNE 14

Jesus himself gives a supreme example of this. He really didn't care much what people thought of him. He didn't care whether they praised him or censured him. He wasn't looking for human approval at all and had no interest in being popular. That doesn't mean that Jesus didn't care about other people; it just meant that their judgment of him didn't carry much weight—he was much more concerned with what God thought of him. And so Jesus was free to say what needed to be said and to do what needed to be done. He didn't trample other people's feelings, nor did he allow human respect to keep him from doing the right thing.

Jesus knew that many times we fail to do the right thing for fear of what others will think or say. For example, in his gospel, St. John comments sadly on some Pharisees who honestly believed in Jesus but never became his disciples for fear they would be put out of the synagogue. And he adds, "they loved human glory more than the glory that comes from God" (Jn 12:43). This is the big problem with vanity and human respect: we start caring more about people's opinions and less about God's.

———◦◦◦◦———

This happens in our own lives as well. How many times do we fail to say what should be said simply because we don't want

97

In which areas of my life do I tend to care more about the respect of other people than the respect of God himself?

to be labeled a "holy Joe"? How many times do we keep our faith silent or compromise our own principles because we don't want to be different from the rest? That's why Jesus reminds us that we are *salt,* and salt is meant to taste different. In fact, he says, if it stops tasting different, it is no longer good for anything (see Mt 5:13)!

On the positive side, too, vanity makes us do things simply for ourselves and for the credit we will receive, rather than out of a pure desire to serve God and neighbor. That's why Jesus invites us to quickly forget about our own good deeds and to stop looking for praise. He uses a bodily example: "Do not let your left hand know what your right hand is doing" (Mt 6:3). He is referring specifically to almsgiving, but the maxim can be applied to many aspects of our life. Any time we are tempted to twist our good actions around for personal gain, we should hear the words of Jesus resounding in our soul. He reminds us that we don't need that extra motivation. The Father's love is enough for us!

Lord, what a beautiful example you give me! It is impressive to see your purity of intention. When I look at your life, I realize that you weren't in it for yourself but for us. All your efforts, all your sacrifices, all your labors, all your struggles were not for you; they were for me! Since your love was pure, you were free to always do the right thing for the right reason. You loved simply, honestly, and without any second intentions. Thank you!

I know that I care too much for what others think of me. I desire their praise and their esteem, their affection and their appreciation. When I do something good for someone I like it to be recognized and feel hurt when I am not thanked. I also avoid situations where I could look stupid or uncool, and sometimes I don't do what I should because I am afraid of what others will think of me. I am still a long way from where you want me to be!

Lord, I think the key is a greater love for God. If I realize that I am always in his presence and that his opinion is the only one that really counts, it will be easier for me to act with purity of inten-

tion. Let me love people very much but not care too much for what they think of me. I know I can't please everyone, and the one I ultimately want to please is you!

———◆◆◆———

Jesus, unpretentious of heart,
make my heart more like yours!

JUNE 15

A prayerful HEART

"Abba, Father!"
Mk 14:36

You might think that being God, Jesus would have been pretty self-sufficient. There wasn't much he *couldn't* do, after all. He walked on water, cured lepers, calmed storms, and even raised the dead. So why pray? What need could Jesus possibly have had to talk to God? Or was it just playacting, "pretending" to talk to his Father?

To understand this better, maybe we should review our understanding of what God is really like. People sometimes have a rather unchristian idea of a solitary god, sitting high on Mount Olympus or Valhalla, lost in his own thoughts. This secluded god, this distant "unmoved mover" isn't the God Jesus revealed to us, and it doesn't reflect Jesus' life, either.

When I pray, what is my primary motivation?

Jesus revealed a God who was a trinity of persons, a community rather than an isolated individual. And Jesus, as man, lived this communion with his Father, especially through *prayer*. When Jesus went off to the mountain or the desert, he wasn't "lost in his own thoughts" but immersed in conversation with his Father. He loved his Father and because of this, he loved to spend time with him. For Jesus, prayer wasn't a chore he had to get out of the way but a delight, an activity that he relished and looked forward to. That's why so often in the gospel we find Jesus engaged in prayer. He made time for prayer because for him, it was a priority.

In short, Jesus didn't pray just because he "needed" to. He didn't turn to God just as a problem-solver or a bodyguard. He turned to him as a *Father*. It would be a shame if the only time we dealt with our father was when we needed to borrow the car keys or take out a short-term loan! This wasn't Jesus' attitude. He bounced ideas off God, shared his innermost thoughts and aspirations with him, and sometimes just enjoyed his company without saying anything at all. So we find Jesus praising his Father, thanking him, pleading with him, and spending hours in his presence. The heart of Jesus was indeed a prayerful heart.

———•◆•———

The truly amazing thing is that we are all called to this intimate communion with God. What do you make of these words, spoken by Christ to the Father at the Last Supper? "As you, Father, are in me and I am in you, may they also be in us" (Jn 17:21). He asks God that we, too, may enjoy the same type of intimacy with him that the Father and the Son share! A moment later Jesus repeats a similar thought: "I in them and you in me, that they may become completely one, so that the world may know that you have sent me and have loved them even as you have loved me" (Jn 17:23).

Jesus assures us that he wills this level of communion with us. God invites us into his own intimacy, into communion with the Blessed Trinity. This is undoubtedly a lot for us to swallow or even to begin to understand, but we should try. It tells us a lot about who we are and who we were meant to be.

What excuses do I tend to make when I don't feel like spending time with God in prayer?

Prayer can be hard work, it is true. It requires perseverance and effort, sometimes even just to keep focused on what we are doing. But it is an exercise that can change our lives. God doesn't settle for a mere platonic relationship with us, or a passing acquaintance. He wants our friendship. He wants our intimacy. He wants our trust. He wants our company. Like Jesus, we need to *make* time to devote to God. Prayer doesn't just happen; we need to make it happen. There is no better use of our time.

Lord, in the midst of your countless activities, you found an extraordinary amount of time to spend with your Father. You valued prayer and made it a priority. You didn't just think of praying when you needed something from God but carried on an active relationship of love with him. You liked to be with him, and made him your deepest confidant. You spoke with him of your most personal thoughts, frustrations, doubts, and ideals. Thank you for this example!

I understand the value of prayer in theory, but in practice I often find it difficult. Sometimes I don't see that it changes very much. Did you ever experience that? It would help me to know that it wasn't always easy for you either. Did you always feel God's presence? Did you get immediate answers to all your doubts and questions? I bet you didn't, but I'm sure this didn't diminish your trust in him or your steadfastness in your prayer.

Lord, help me to appreciate prayer. Help me to be more grateful for the honor of being able to speak with God every day, knowing that he hears me, that he loves me, that he enjoys our time together. Everything looks different from the perspective of prayer because it is your perspective on things from heaven. Teach me to pray as you prayed, in a way that pleases God and draws me into your intimacy.

—◦◦◦◦◦◦—

Prayerful heart of Jesus,
make my heart more like yours!

june 16

A radical HEART

"Get behind me, Satan!"
Mt. 16:23

As gentle as Jesus was, he didn't mince words. Flattery didn't work with him because he saw the truth of things and wasn't deceived by appearances or pretty words. False compassion didn't move him either, if it tempted him away from his mission. So even with people he was close to, Jesus could be very tough. St. Peter learned this the hard way.

If you recall the scene, Jesus had just paid Simon Peter a tremendous compliment, and entrusted him with an important mission. Peter had declared Jesus to be the Messiah, the son of the living God, and Jesus had responded that Peter was blessed, because he had learned this from his heavenly Father. And he declared Simon Peter to be the "rock" upon which Jesus would build his Church, and promised him the keys to his Kingdom. Peter was riding high!

But then, the topic of conversation changed. Jesus started talking about his passion, and the fact that he would have to go up to Jerusalem to suffer and be put to death. This was too much for Peter, who took Jesus aside and tried to convince him that this was an awful plan. "God forbid it, Lord! This must never happen to you" (Mt 16:22). And then Jesus uttered those terrible words: "Get behind me, Satan! You are a stumbling block to me; for you are setting your mind not on divine things but on human things" (Mt 16:23).

One minute Jesus is praising Peter to the heavens, and the next moment he calls him a devil. What had happened? Why the abrupt change in Jesus' tone? Where did his affection for Peter go? Had he lost his trust in him? Not at all. Jesus loved Peter, but he didn't let his affection for him hinder the fulfillment of God's will. What Peter was proposing seemed very attractive, but Jesus saw it as a temptation, and he reacted fiercely. Peter was suggesting that Jesus shouldn't accept the cross, that he should find another easier way. But this was not the Father's will.

Jesus was incredibly radical when it came to God's will. He didn't allow negotiations with other possibilities. God's will was not one possible option but the only road. It was Jesus' food (see Jn 4:34)! When the devil tries to tempt Jesus in the desert into considering other alternatives, Jesus responds peremptorily, excluding all dialogue. He isn't looking for the easiest path, or even the one that seems most effective. He wants to do things the Father's way.

When have I let the attraction of something "good" lead me away from something "better"—namely, what God was asking of me through his commandments, inspirations, or Church teaching?

Jesus recommends the same radicalness to his disciples. "If your right eye causes you to sin," Jesus says, "tear it out and throw it away; it is better for you to lose one of your members than for your whole body to be thrown into hell" (Mt 5:29). This wasn't the common ground, have-your-cake-and-eat-it-too approach.

It was the yes-or-no, with-me-or-against-me approach. Anything that contradicts God's will isn't worth having around. Jesus could be extremely indulgent with sinners, extremely understanding of human weakness, but he simply accepted no opposition to the Father's will.

During a typical day, how often do I think about "God's will," about what God wants me to do right now, and in what way he wants me to do it?

We are used to compromise in our lives. In a democratic society, there is a necessary give and take. This works well in most areas of our life, but Jesus shows us that there is one area where no compromise should be accepted: God's will. No matter what the cost, no matter what we may have to lose or give up, nothing should stand in the way of what the Father asks of us. This is the road to holiness, and we find it in the lives of all the saints and martyrs. Nothing, not even the fear of death, should make us unfaithful to God.

We rarely face such life-and-death situations in our modern world. Not many of us will be put to the ultimate test of faith. Yet all of us face more subtle trials, where God's will gets heavy and compromise would be easier. It seems so much more "reasonable" to negotiate than to stick to our guns. And here Jesus' example fortifies and enlightens us. All other good things—friendship, family, feelings, personal comfort, even our own lives—must be absolutely secondary to the one thing that really matters: God's will.

Lord, thank you for your example of radicalness. I live in a pluralistic world where compromise is king, where "convictions" and "principles" are considered enemies of peaceful coexistence. But you show me that some things are worth fighting for, even dying for. Absolutes do exist—lines that must not be crossed, alternatives that must not be considered, options that cannot be thrown into the mix. Send me your Holy Spirit to see clearly when I must take this kind of a stand. Let me be courageous in the face of opposition, even when it comes from the people I love most!

I know, Lord, that in many things, compromise is important, and open-mindedness is a true virtue. There is no sense in insisting always on my own opinion, especially in little things. On the other hand, there are issues where you want me to take a stand. I am called not only to be faithful myself but also to bear witness to you and to strengthen my brothers and sisters with my example.

Let me love God's will above all other things. His will gives meaning to my life and expresses his personal love for me. He wants only good things for me, and even when I don't see clearly, help me to trust in his wisdom. Let me call temptation by its name and unmask the enemy of my soul, no matter what guise he puts on. Be my light, and let me be a light for others!

Heart of Jesus, radically committed to the Father's will,
make my heart more like yours!

JUNE 17

A realistic HEART

"What does it profit a man?"
Mk 14:36

Growing up in the 1960s and 1970s, my generation saw Jesus as a hippy leader, a beatnik hero who stood up to "the man." He was a nature lover who was against big government, big cities, and big business. There was an ounce of truth in this stereotype, but also a pound of lies. Jesus was quite simply pro-human. He didn't hate institutions or authority, cities or business, but he knew that to be effective, these things must serve the human person.

How would I describe to an agnostic friend the difference between "eternity-based realism" and "earthly-based realism"?

Oddly, in many ways Jesus reveals a businessman's personality. He often reasoned in terms of costs and benefits, investments, and yield. He expected his disciples to bear fruit and looked for a return on the talents he bestowed. He was not some wide-eyed idealist but a firmly grounded realist. At the same time, Jesus' style of realism was eternity-based and not earthly. He encouraged his followers to discover the true value of things and to pursue the ones that counted in the long run. He says, for instance, that we shouldn't run around worried about small potatoes like what we are to eat and what we are to drink but to set our hearts on bigger things, like his kingdom (see Mt 6:31-33).

This realism reaches a head in Jesus' well-known saying: "For what will it profit a man if he gain the whole world but forfeits his life? Or what will he give in return for his life?" (Mt 16:26). Note well that Jesus doesn't ask us not to look for profit but rather to look for *real* profit, where it matters. He invites us to be reasonable, to consider what investments are really worth the trouble and what ones aren't. This same thread runs through many of his other teachings as well. He says, for example, "Do not store up for yourselves treasures on earth, where moth and rust consume and where thieves break in and steal." What would be the point in amassing a fortune that is so precarious, and so subject to loss?

If someone observed my normal behavior for a week, where would they conclude I am "storing up my treasure," on earth or in heaven?

And so he goes on: "Store up for yourselves treasures in heaven, where neither moth nor rust consumes and where thieves do not break in and steal. For where your treasure is, there your heart will be also" (Mt 6:19-21). This is realism. This is the eternal logic that Christ proposes to his followers.

Jesus lived according to this code. He didn't waste time with investments that weren't going to yield an eternal profit. Every minute of his life was spent in more fruitful pursuits, with an eye ever on the bottom line: the salvation of souls. Jesus knew what was important, and never deviated from his course. No amount of glitter or passing attractions could pull him away from this path. For Jesus, it was God's criteria (not the world's) and people (not things). It was as simple as that!

Because of this, eternal goods always trumped temporal goods in Jesus' life. He would never trade an eternal benefit for a merely earthly gain. In the Letter to the Hebrews we read that Jesus endured the cross "for the sake of the joy that was set before him" (Heb 12:2). He lived in his own flesh the motto that St. Paul would later adopt: "I consider that the sufferings of this present time are not worth comparing with the glory about to be revealed to us" (Rom 8:18). No matter how many earthly treasures we pile up, they can never equal heaven. No matter how many sorrows we may have to endure in this short life, they can never come close to outweighing the glory of eternal life with God!

In our own lives, this scale of values can easily be turned on its head. We may think we have good business sense, but we sometimes make terrible deals, taking a tiny short-term gain and losing out on lasting treasures. There is an eerie sixteenth-century hymn that

Write down your "scale of values": What are the five most important realities in your life, in order of importance? What are you willing to sacrifice and suffer in order to maintain this scale of values?

is still sung sometimes during Holy Week. This sacred motet is titled *Judas Mercator Pessimus* (Judas, the Worst of Merchants) and reminds us how Judas made a monstrous deal, trading in his Savior for thirty pieces of silver. It is meant to remind us to be smart in our business deals, accumulating treasure that will last, pearls of great price that no one can ever take away.

Lord, you saw things very clearly. You kept your priorities straight, even when tempted by tantalizing offers or threatened with horrible punishments. You knew that eternity is what counts in the long run. You were the model businessman, immune to shysters who offered cheap products and attentive to the true value of things. Thank you for this example of clarity and business sense!

I like to consider myself a realist, but often I get taken in by attractive offers that aren't worth the price I am made to pay. Help me recognize the true value of things, and to keep my priorities as clear as yours. Above all, help me value heaven more than anything I can acquire on earth. Remind me often that everything here us passing, and only heaven lasts forever.

Heart of Jesus, realistic in your pursuits, make my heart more like yours!

JUNE 18

A simple HEART

"Let the little children come to me."
Mt 19:14

Jesus is rightly considered the greatest teacher that ever lived. His wisdom went beyond that of Socrates or Plato, Confucius or Einstein. Yet, despite the undeniable depth of his message, he taught with astonishing simplicity. Most of his teaching took the form of parables—simple stories that even uneducated people could understand. He made the message of salvation accessible to everyone, the learned and unlearned alike.

How much of an influence does it have on my opinion of someone when I find out that they went to a prestigious university? How much influence should it have?

In our modern world, education and sophistication are highly prized commodities. We assume that the more degrees and titles a person possesses, the greater that person is and the better he grasps the true meaning of human life. In our ranking of persons, academic achievements count for much. As Christians, however, we should ask ourselves whether this way of assessing people corresponds to what Jesus did and taught. How impressed was Jesus with the "wisdom" of this world?

Not much, it would seem. In fact, his idea of greatness took an altogether different tack. You will recall the quarrel that broke out among the twelve apostles regarding who among them was the greatest. James and John, the sons of Zebedee, had already approached Jesus to try to shore up key "Cabinet seats" in Jesus' future kingdom, and this had obviously irked the others. So once in the house, Jesus asks the apostles what they had been discussing along the way. They fell silent because they were ashamed to tell him they had been arguing about which of them was the most important. So Jesus said to them:

"Whoever wants to be first must be last of all and servant of all" (Mk 9:35). Then he took a little child and put it among them; taking it in his arms, he said to them, "Whoever welcomes one such child in my name welcomes me, and whoever welcomes me welcomes not me but the one who sent me" (Mk 9:37).

Interestingly, Jesus doesn't seem to mind that the apostles were ambitious. He doesn't reproach them for desiring greatness or for wanting to be all they could be. Rather, he invites them to set their sights even higher, to where true greatness lies. But the paradox is that in order to go higher, they need to go lower. Jesus' model for greatness is not Bill Gates, Michael Jordan, King Herod, or Julius Caesar. It is about as unlikely as it could be: a small child, with no rank and no accomplishments to his name. He tells us that if we really wish to be something, we need to choose the last place and become servants of our brothers and sisters.

Why is it so hard for us to "choose the last place" and serve our brothers and sisters without looking for anything in return?

Once again, Jesus doesn't just preach; he practices. He is as simple as simple can be—no special titles, no degrees, no dignities, no rank. He's just a teacher from a small town, busy saving

Use your imagination to picture what it might have been like to walk up to Jesus on the streets of Galilee and ask him for advice.

the world. He is comfortable with rich and poor, men and women, adults and children, politicians and fishermen. He doesn't require an appointment to speak with him, or special references. People come forward and ask him favors with no fear of rejection. He inspires confidence and closeness because his heart is simple. Not that Jesus minded important titles or worldly accomplishments—it's just that these things didn't seem to impress him very much.

Jesus himself says that the Son of Man did not come into the world to be served but to serve (see Mt 20:28). This is what we see in his day-to-day life. People don't wait on him hand and foot, take him out to fancy restaurants, or engage him on costly speaking tours. No royal court surrounds him, and no secret service men hold people away from him. He doesn't set up shop on the forty-ninth floor at a Jerusalem office suite to await posh visitors; he goes out to meet people, to listen, to heal, to serve. This is the simplicity that marks his life and his heart.

Alas, we often aren't like this. We thrive on meeting celebrities and hanging out with high rollers. We love stories about friends meeting presidents or running into movie stars in an airport. We still associate greatness with worldly renown, celebrity status, athletic prowess, or

What kind of greatness am I aspiring to? (Be honest.)

impressive achievements. Rarely would we spontaneously look at a little child and think: "Ah! I am in the presence of true greatness!" There's nothing wrong with fame or human accomplishments, of course. Like the apostles, however, we need to learn that there is a higher form of greatness to esteem and aspire to.

Lord, I live in a world that has a strange set of values. Things that are worthless in your sight are prized highly, and things that you admire are scoffed at or ignored. Unfortunately, I sometimes live caught up between these two worlds, so although I want to be fully "Christian" in my outlook, I am easily swept along by much more worldly criteria. St. Paul said that the world as we know it is "passing away" (1 Cor 7:31), but it is the only world I know. You call me to live in this world without being of the world. You want

me to set a tone for those around me, rather than taking on the tone of my surroundings. Help me to do this!

Thank you for your moving example of simplicity. You walked among people—the great and the small—without losing your bearings. You loved each one, without getting caught up in who they were or what they had achieved. How our world could use a good dose of your simplicity! How I could!

In order to acquire a simple heart, I will need to care less about worldly opinion. I will need to focus on what is important in your eyes, and what you consider to be great. I know that there is a lot of this greatness around me—simple people who live beautiful lives, hidden in their daily fidelity and salt-of-the-earth goodness. Give me eyes to notice them and a heart to appreciate them.

———

Jesus, simple of heart,
make my heart more like yours!

JUNE 19

A grateful HEART

"I thank you, Father."
Mk 11:25

As little children, all of us are taught to say "please" and "thank you." We learn that courtesy and politeness are important, and they characterize us as well mannered. As life goes on, however, we realize that true gratitude goes much deeper than mere courtesy. It is a virtue of the heart and a very rare one at that.

Everyone asks for favors, but few remember to thank. We beg profusely when we need something, but our thanks are

When was the last time I said "thank you" and really, really meant it?

brief and formalistic. This was Jesus' experience, too, and it reveals an important quality of his heart.

One day, when Jesus was traveling through the region between Samaria and Galilee, ten lepers rushed up to meet him (see Lk 17:11-19). From a safe distance, they shouted out, "Jesus, Master, have mercy on us!" Immediately, Jesus

When was the last time someone really thanked me from their heart, and how did it make me feel?

sent them off to show themselves to the priests. They did so, but on the way, they realized that they had been healed. Here, something quite typical happened. Overjoyed with this tremendous miracle, most of the men ran off to tell their families and friends. They were overcome by their good fortune and wanted to share the news with their loved ones. One of the men, however, went running back to Jesus. He praised God with a loud voice and threw himself at Jesus' feet and thanked him.

Jesus looked down at the man and asked, "Were not ten made clean? But the other nine, where are they?" (Lk 17:17). He found it strange that only one of the men had come back to thank God, since all had received the same marvelous grace. Surely, in part, he was sad because he still had more to give. This miracle was just a sign and foretaste of the truly great things he wanted to do for these men. Yet only one came back, and this one received the gift of faith. But this scene also gives us a glimpse into Jesus' heart, and how he appreciated the noble virtue of gratitude.

In his own dealings, especially with God, Jesus exhibits this virtue over and over. We have already seen how, before healing Lazarus, Jesus says, "Father, I thank you for hearing me." But he also gives thanks before every meal, and thanks God for revealing to little ones what is hidden from the learned and the clever (see Lk 10:21). We sometimes think that God's blessings are to be expected, but Jesus never took them for granted. He took the time to thank God because he had a grateful heart.

In his dealings with us, too, Jesus is just as grateful. During his earthly life as well as now, he is deeply grateful for every gesture of love and every act of kindness. Nothing is lost on him. He may forget our faults and failings, but he never

Think of some little thing you can do for Jesus today—something that will please him—then resolve to do it.

forgets our acts of affection for him (which include all those things done for the "least" of his brothers and sisters). This is deeply consoling, when we realize that many of our attempts at kindness are lost on the people they are meant to serve. Jesus remembers! One day, he will display before us the many gestures of love that we offered him during our lives, many of which we ourselves will have forgotten. And he will say "thank you" with an eternal embrace.

<hr />

Knowing how much gratitude pleases the heart of Christ, there are many ways we can grow in this virtue daily. The little kindnesses all around us, which we so easily take for granted, furnish us with constant opportunities to thank. The humbler we are and the more aware of our own unworthiness of the many gifts we daily receive, the easier we will find it to practice this beautiful quality of Jesus' heart.

God's gifts are meant to lead us to him, not away from him. The same created things can be an occasion for growing in gratitude and love or an occasion to turn away from God preferring his gifts. In his marvelous book *The Imitation of Christ*, Thomas à Kempis puts these wise words into Jesus' mouth:

> "Be grateful, therefore, for the least gift and you will be worthy to receive a greater. Consider the least gift as the greatest, the most contemptible as something special. And, if you but look to the dignity of the Giver, no gift will appear too small or worthless."

Lord, I am often more aware of the good things I do for others than of the good things they do for me. It almost seems expected that people treat me well. I also take God's many gifts to me for granted. Let me start right now to thank you as you deserve.

Thank you for creating me, for calling me into existence. I was nothing, and would never have been, unless you had loved me and desired that I exist. Thank you for my parents and for the education I received from them and so many others, especially those who taught me most about you. Thank you for the amazing gift of faith and for my baptism, by which I know who you are and why I am here on earth.

Thank you for my friends and family, for my teachers and mentors. Thank you for the good books that I have read, the music that lifts my heart to you, and the beautiful creation that surrounds me. Thank you for sunsets and forests and beaches and mountains. Thank you for thunderstorms and soft sunshine, for hot showers and cool breezes.

Thank you, Jesus, for becoming a human being like me. Thank you for your example of obedience, of purity, of gentleness, of strength of character. Thank you for suffering and dying for me, for saving me from my sins. Thank you for founding the Church, so that I, along with so many others, could encounter you.

———— ❖•❖•❖ ————

Heart of Jesus, grateful to God and others,
make my heart more like yours!

JUNE 20

A **joyful** HEART

"That my joy may be in you."
Jn 15:11

One of the enduring negative myths about Jesus paints him as a spoilsport. The legend has it that God saw us humans having too much fun, so he sent his son down to earth to make things more complicated for us, including a bunch of rules to obey. After having us jump through all these moral hoops, God would reward us with heaven.

As we probably know from personal experience, this story doesn't hold up. Far from looking to make our life more difficult, Jesus came to offer us the fullness of life. He saw us enslaved and came as our liberator. He saw us lost and came to show us the way home. He saw us confused and brought us the truth. He saw us lonely and forsaken and came to show us a Father's love. But he also came to bring us joy. He saw us sad, frustrated, anxious, and fearful and came to share his own happiness with us.

To what extent am I drawn to spending time with Jesus, to basking in his company? Why am I not drawn to him more intensely?

It's true that the Gospel doesn't offer instances of Jesus breaking down in fits of laughter, playing pranks on the apostles, or telling jokes around the campfire. We find him weeping at times but never guffawing. At the same time, the portrait of Jesus we get from the Gospel tells of a joyful heart, drawing those around him to discover what he had inside. We know, for instance, that children are naturally repelled by grouches, yet we find them clustering around Jesus and basking in his company. People were happy to be with Jesus because his own interior joy was contagious.

We read that Jesus "rejoiced in the Holy Spirit" (Lk 10:21). He tells his apostles to ask in order to receive, "so that your joy may be complete" (Jn 16:24). He says that after the pain of his passion is over, "your hearts will rejoice, and no one will take your joy from you" (Jn 16:22). Perhaps even more tellingly, Jesus tells them he has taught them about the Father's love "so that my joy may be in you, and that your joy may be complete" (Jn 15:11). It was *his own joy* he promised to share with them, a participation in his own serenely joyful heart.

Why was Jesus joyful? In the midst of so many travails with the weight of the world's salvation upon his shoul-

When I stop to think about the Father's love for me, what sentiment crops up in my heart?

ders, what was there to rejoice about? Surely what brought him the greatest joy was the Father's love—the realization that no matter what, the Father would be by his side as his light and his strength. Nothing could ever separate him from the Father's love. He rejoiced in the simple goodness of children, in the beauty of conversion, in the knowledge that he was opening the doors of salvation to a countless multitude of his brothers and sisters.

How often do I give the gift of a smile to others, even though I may be feeling down myself?

If our hearts are to be like Christ's, they must be filled with this same joy. Sulkiness and Christianity have never gone well together, borne out by St. Teresa's saying that "a sad saint is a sorry saint." Our deep joy reveals the authenticity of our encounter with the Risen Lord and becomes an invitation to others to discover what we have found. This joy is so important that St. Paul turns it into a command for Christians: "Rejoice in the Lord always; again I will say, Rejoice!" (Phil 4:4). In this way, joy becomes not just a passive feeling that comes and goes but a true Christian virtue, something to "practice." Our smile becomes a gift to others. Just think of Mother Teresa of Calcutta, whose smile lit up the world, despite the internal darkness that characterized much of her life.

And our motivation for joy must also be similar to Christ's. It isn't a fiction, a painted-on clown's smile, hiding inner angst. It doesn't come and go with the waves of personal fortune. It issues forth from within, from the knowledge that we, too, are loved with an everlasting love. Like St. Paul, we, too, must be "convinced that neither death, nor life, nor angels, nor rulers, nor things present, nor things to come, nor powers, nor height, nor depth, nor anything else in all creation, will be able to separate us from the love of God in Christ Jesus our Lord" (Rom 8:38-39). If this is our heartfelt conviction, what could possibly tarnish our joy?

Lord Jesus, how I would have loved to meet you here on earth. Your personality was so attractive, your character so magnetizing, that everyone wanted to be with you. Above all I would have liked to experience the deep joy that filled you. I would have liked to see you smile. Teach me to smile like that, to offer your smile to the world.

I often look for joy in the wrong places. I easily confuse passing mirth or frivolity with true happiness. But these things depart as fast as they came and often leave only sadness and emptiness in their wake. The joy I seek doesn't come and go. In your words, it becomes a fountain within, welling up to eternal life. I want the true joy that comes from knowing you, experiencing your goodness and living by your grace. Then come what may, I will hold the key to everlasting happiness.

Make me, Lord, an apostle of joy. In a world filled with anguish and vanity, people hunger and thirst for the joy that only you can give. I must bear witness to my faith and my hope through joy, so that everyone will want to know you, too. Let joy be the gift I offer to others, and to you as well, since you love a cheerful giver!

———————

Jesus, joyful of heart,
make my heart more like yours!

JUNE 21

A reassuring HEART

*"Do not let your hearts
be troubled."*

Jn 14:1

Jesus refers to himself as the Good Shepherd who knows and
defends his sheep. Looking over Jerusalem, he likewise compares
himself to a mother hen: "How often have I desired to gather
your children together as a hen gathers her brood under her
wings!" (Mt 23:37). In his

heart, Jesus feels a desire to

protect us, to gather us to

himself, and to take care of

*How comfortable am I with
the idea that God wants to
console me with a mother's
care?*

us. This solicitude is almost maternal, similar to what we read of our relationship with God in Psalm 131: "I hold myself in quiet and silence, like a little child in its mother's arms, like a little child, so I keep myself" (Ps 131:2 NJB).

At the Last Supper, soon to be taken prisoner and condemned to death, Jesus consoles his disciples as if they were his children. He knows that the next hours will be extremely trying for them. He puts his own fear aside for a moment and seeks to comfort them and reassure them. He warns them of what will happen, so that when it comes to pass they will take courage and not lose heart. Here, in this moment of crisis, we find some of the tenderest words in the entire Gospel.

"Do not let your hearts be troubled," he says. "Believe in God, believe also in me" (Jn 14:1). He doesn't want his own passion to be a stumbling block for them or an obstacle to their faith in God or in him. Jesus' heart was so big that all he could think of in this terrible moment was the good of his friends who had stood by him. He goes on to say, "In my Father's house, there are many dwelling places. If it were not so, would I have told you that I go to prepare a place for you? And if I go and prepare a place for you, I will come again and will take you to myself,

so that where I am, there you may be also" (Jn. 14:2-3). He sets
their hearts on heaven to help them through a terrible ordeal.

You are probably familiar with the beautiful prayer attrib-
uted to St. Francis of Assisi, a prayer that begins "Make me
an instrument of your peace." In the second strophe of the
poem, Francis prays the following: "O Divine Master, grant
that I may not so much seek to be consoled as to console; to
be understood, as to understand; to be loved, as to love." These
words are a description of Jesus' heart. Even in his darkest hour
he looked to console rather than be consoled, to understand
rather than be understood, to love rather than be loved. His
was truly a reassuring heart, a
maternal heart whispering
to his children: *Don't worry.*
Everything will be all right.

When have I experienced
God comforting me? Why
do I not experience it more
often?

After speaking these reassuring words to his disciples, Jesus
begins to talk to his Father, and his heartfelt prayer bears the
same solicitude. He is afraid to leave his children, not because of
his own pain, but out of concern for them. So he says, "While
I was with them, I protected them in your name that you have
given me. I guarded them, and not one of them was lost except

the one destined to be lost" (Jn. 14:12). He turns them over to his Father's care, confident in the power of his love. "I am not asking you to take them out of the world, but I ask you to protect them from the evil one" (Jn 14:15). How striking that at a time when Jesus would seem most justified in praying for himself, he utters this poignant prayer for others!

Right now, who in my life needs to be comforted, and what can I do about it?

Our natural selfishness makes this tough for us. When we are overwhelmed by our own problems and fears, it is tremendously difficult to think of others and their needs. Jesus was surely able to do this because he had formed the habit of placing others first. He naturally considered their needs before his own and focused his attention on reassuring those around him, rather than on his own real difficulties.

All of us, men or women, are called to develop this maternal and paternal dimension of our hearts. We are called to watch over those around us, bolster their confidence, console them, and accompany them through their trials. Sometimes even

when we feel weakest, God will give us the grace to be a source
of strength for those who are still weaker.

*Lord, when I contemplate your example of tenderness and
warmth, I am moved with gratitude. Thank you for this example, and thank you still more for being there for me in my own
life, to console me in my struggles and embolden me in my time of
doubt. You are indeed a brother to me but also, in a way, a father
and mother. You know my needs better than I do and care for
my interests even more than I. Nothing escapes you. Everything
about me matters to you. Thank you!*

*Is there any way I can be like this with those around me? Can I,
too, be a source of consolation and comfort for the many troubled
souls that I come into contact with each day? I am sure you want
this of me. I am sure that you would like others to encounter your
loving heart through their contact with me. I know that one of the
most convincing ways of preaching your Gospel is simply by loving
others. In true Christian love, souls meet you.*

My prayer for today is this: let me, too, seek to love better rather than to be loved. Give me the gift of understanding and less concern for being understood. Grant me the grace of being a consolation for others and less desirous of finding consolation in them. You will be my prize. You will be my strength. You will be my comfort.

Jesus, reassuring of heart,
make my heart more like yours!

JUNE 22

A **courageous** HEART

*"Jesus resolutely set out
for Jerusalem."*
Lk 9:51

We sometimes think of Jesus as being inexorably drawn by fate toward his passion and death. He seems almost like a victim— albeit a willing one—of destiny, without much say in the matter. For this reason, it is easy to undervalue the courage it took for him to be faithful.

Jesus did his best to eliminate this misunderstanding. He said, "I lay down my life in order to take it up again. No one takes it

In my mind, how do I define courage? What does it look like in my imagination?

from me, but I lay it down of my own accord. I have power to lay it down, and I have power to take it up again" (Jn 10:17-18). He wanted us to understand that his sacrifice was free. He chose to give his life for us, out of love for us and love for the Father. That's why in the Garden of Gethsemani, when Peter steps forward to defend Jesus from the guards who have come to take him into custody, Jesus tells him to put away his sword. He asks Peter: "Do you think that I cannot appeal to my Father, and he will at once send me more than twelve legions of angels?" (Mt 26:53). In other words, if he was captured, it's because he allowed himself to be captured. At any moment, he could have called it off. At any moment, he could have said no.

Jesus' absolute freedom underscores the power of his courage. He could have walked away, but he didn't. And though his passion and death provide the best example of this courageous heart, we see it all through his life. He was courageous when he had to leave his beloved home and mother to begin his public mission. He was courageous when he faced hostile crowds, seeking to throw him off a cliff. He was courageous when he taught the undiluted truth, despite the negative consequences. He was courageous when argu-

Whom do I know personally who has shown truly Christlike courage?

ing with the scribes and Pharisees, knowing that they were plotting his death. And yes, he was courageous before the Sanhedrin, before Herod, before Pontius Pilate, and before his executioners. He never fled from hardship or from persecution or from sacrifice. Because he had such remarkable courage, nothing and no one would change his course.

Courage is often undervalued in the Christian life. Yet oftentimes we fail to accom-

What are my biggest fears in life?

plish the good we set out to do not because we don't want to, but because we lack the courage to see the project through. Often it is fear that paralyzes our good intentions, and makes them sterile and fruitless. We don't pray because it's hard and we see no results. We don't ask pardon for our sins, because we lack the courage to face up to them. We don't persevere in our good resolutions because to do so requires sacrifice. And we don't follow Jesus too closely because it means embracing the cross. If only we had more courage!

We rightly associate courage with the witness of the martyrs. It took extreme courage to accept death rather than betray God and their faith in him. We rightly gaze with admiration at the courage of even little children—like St. Agnes or St. Tarcisius or St. Maria Goretti—who showed such astonishing courage in the face of torment and death. But really, courage is necessary for every Christian heart. It is never a smooth, well-trodden path that we are called to travel, "for the gate is narrow and the road is hard that leads to life, and there are few who find it" (Mt 7:14).

Which of the two types of courage do I need more right now?

The strange thing is that love itself requires courage. Jesus taught that we will never learn what love is and never bear fruit unless we learn to die to ourselves. Jesus was courageous because he loved much. His love for the Father's will and for each of us gave him a superhuman courage that permitted him to overcome even the most daunting of obstacles. St. Thomas Aquinas said that courage is necessary for two things: to undertake difficult enterprises and to be patient in bearing suffering. Jesus had this courage in spades. The tenderness of his heart didn't make him soft, and the staunchness of his heart didn't make him insensi-tive. His heart bore the perfect harmony of love in all its dimensions.

We, too, are free. We, too, can say yes or no to God. We, too, can escape many difficulties and inconveniences if we choose to. But with God's grace we can also be faithful regardless of the cost.

Lord, the more I study your life, the more impressed I am by the completeness of your character. The better I get to know you the more I appreciate the beauty of virtue the way you revealed and lived it. You make me love you more, and you make me want to be like you.

At the same time, all of this frightens me. It seems to go beyond what I feel capable of. The ideal is so high that I really don't think I can reach it. It almost seems that I need courage just to want to be courageous! I have so many fears, so many doubts, so much timidity where I should have strength.

I know that the key is a deeper union with you, so that I don't think of myself apart from you, as if I were just imitating you the way I would imitate somebody else's example. You really want to live in me, to make your virtue my virtue and your love my love. I want that too! I need your grace, I need your courage!

When I think of those little ten-year-old martyrs, I realize that it isn't human strength that emboldens the Christian heart. It is your Holy Spirit. St. Paul said: "It is no longer I who live, but it is Christ who lives in me" (Gal 2:20). That's what I need—for you to live in me.

———◆◆◆———

Jesus, bold and courageous of heart,
make my heart more like yours!

JUNE 23

AN **obedient** HEART

"Whatever the Father does,
the Son does likewise."

Jn 5:19

Some like to think of Jesus as a first-century Che Guevara, a sort of proto-Marxist revolutionary, rebelling against the leaders of his day and forging a new path for religion. He knew his mind, to be sure, and didn't let others move him if he didn't want to be moved. At the same time, Jesus didn't seek nonconformity for its own sake. And when it came to the Father's will, Jesus wasn't a revolutionary at all.

When I think of the word "obedience," what images and feelings does it conjure up? Why?

We easily forget that Jesus saved us by his *obedience*. His heart was fully, totally tuned into the Father's will as the guiding light for his decisions. Ever since the Nuremburg trials ("I was only following orders"), the concept of obedience has gotten a bad reputation. It can seem subhuman, uncreative, robotic, and downright unpleasant. But we'll never understand Jesus' heart without it. For Jesus, obedience was none of these things. It was, quite simply, an expression of his love for God. More than anything else in the world, he desired to please his Father. His conscience was so clear on this point that he could say, "I always do what is pleasing to him" (Jn 8:29).

Few of us can say that. Sometimes we don't even ask ourselves whether what we are doing *right now* is pleasing to God or not. Sometimes, it's just what we feel like doing. Sometimes, it's what we have to do. Sometimes, we're not even sure why we're doing what we're doing—but Jesus knew. "I always do what is pleasing to him."

This obedience, this conformity with the Father's will, led to imitation. Jesus was united to the Father in everything and found in the Father not only his source of direction but also his model. Jesus wasn't worried about being innova-

When was the last time I asked myself, "What would Jesus do in my situation?"

tive or original. "Very truly, I tell you, the Son can do nothing on his own, but only what he sees the Father doing; for whatever the Father does, the Son does likewise" (Jn 5:19). When we ask ourselves "What would Jesus do?" we find that he was asking himself what the Father would do.

So, when Jesus looks for an example to illustrate what it means to love beyond the demands of strict justice, he turns to the Father: "For he makes his sun rise on the evil and on the good and sends rain on the righteous and on the unrighteous" (Mt 5:45). The same way we look to imitate Christ, he sought to imitate the Father. "My Father goes on working, and so do I" (Jn 5:17).

Like a little boy, Jesus was proud of his Father. He delighted in the Father's works and wanted to be like him. He was unabashedly his "daddy's boy." Jesus didn't seem to feel the need to make his own mark, to get out of the family business to do his own thing. He was the opposite of the prodi-

Why is it that I do not always experience delight when I obey God's commandments?

gal son, who left the Father's house in search of something more exciting. For Jesus, there could be nothing more exciting or wonderful than living in the Father's house and being in the Father's heart. And he willed this same joy for us: "If you keep my commandments, you will abide in my love, just as I have kept my Father's commandments and abide in his love" (Jn 15:10). For Jesus, God's commands weren't an annoying burden; they were his pleasure.

This attitude led Jesus to obey always and spontaneously. He considered doing the Father's will to be his "food" (Jn 4:34), in which he found nourishment and strength. Even when it seemed truly painful and almost incomprehensible, his prayer continued to be: "not my will, but your will be done" (Lk 22:42). And as hard as this could be, Jesus never rebelled. He never seemed to consider doing things any other way. He didn't feel put upon or taken advantage of. He loved the Father, and he also trusted him. He has the utmost confidence, as if to say: "If God asks this of me, it's because he loves me." Truly, God's will was his peace.

Lord, I find joy in contemplating your heart. I love to see how much you loved your Father and how you sought to please him in everything. You were, in many ways, like a little child—like the children you put forward as an example to us all. You didn't question. You didn't revolt or dissent. You simply obeyed with full freedom, full consent, and a heart full of love. Thank you!

I find obedience difficult, to say the least. I hate it when others tell me what to do. I feel like I should be the one to decide what is right for me. And even when I do obey (which I honestly try to do), it seems more like a duty than a joy. I see in your example how love perfects freedom. That the more I love, the freer I will be. I also need to trust more. Sometimes it seems incredibly hard to believe that God has thoroughly thought out the consequences of what he is asking. Does he realize how hard it can be? I know he does, and I know he loves me so much that he would never ask of me or even permit what was not ultimately for my good. Yet it isn't immediately evident. Teach me to trust in him!

Often I have seen that doing things God's way works out for the best. Make my heart more docile, so that the Father's will may become my food, as it was for you. I, too, want to be like him. I want to take him as my model, as you did. After all, I was made in his image and likeness, so how could I have any other pattern for my actions? And let me do this all with joy, the joy of a child in his father's arms.

Jesus, obedient of heart,
make my heart more like yours!

JUNE 24

A **UNIVERSAL** HEART

"Everyone is searching for you."
Mk 1:37

All of us have people we sympathize with and others who rub us the wrong way. This is only natural. Similarities of temperament and common interests quickly bond us to certain individuals, while others come across as less interesting or at times even irritating and unpleasant.

One of the extraordinary qualities of Jesus' heart is its universality. Quite simply, it seemed to have room for everyone. In Jesus' presence, no one felt excluded, or less

Are there individuals or types of people that I tend to exclude from my heart? Why?

important, or unwanted. The embrace of Jesus' heart seemed to envelop the entire world. Because of this, he also brought out the best in people. People became less defensive around him and allowed their hearts to open to his.

Not everyone responded this way, of course. There were those who found Jesus threatening, mostly because he up-ended their way of doing business and challenged them in ways they didn't wish to be challenged. For others, the very openness and universality of Jesus' heart was off-putting, since they espoused a more elitist view of religion and the Kingdom of God. They found his mercy particularly distasteful and wondered aloud how he could justify spending so much time with "sinners."

Yet for the majority, especially the simple, the poor and the

Jesus never rejected a repentant sinner, so why do I sometimes fear being rejected by God?

dispossessed, Jesus' openness was wonderfully refreshing and consoling. He challenged them too, to be sure, and encouraged them to become better. He never justifies wrongdoing, and in his mercy still enjoined them to "go, and sin no more" (Jn 8:11). Yet he did so in such a gentle way, that they found his invitations irresistible.

A particularly memorable example of this was Jesus' encounter with the tax collector Zacchaeus in Jericho (see Lk 19:1-10). Zacchaeus, you will recall, was a short fellow and had to climb a sycamore tree in order to get a look at Jesus as he passed by. Much was his surprise when Jesus approached the very tree where Zacchaeus was installed and called up to him. "Found out" and unable to beat a hasty retreat, Zacchaeus surely feared the worst. He was, after all, a dishonest man, and had heard the reproaches of religious leaders before that point.

Nevertheless, this wasn't what Zacchaeus received from Jesus. Rather than point out Zacchaeus' faults, Jesus calls up to him by name and invites himself over for dinner, as if the two were old friends. "Zacchaeus, hurry and come down; for I must stay at your house today" (Lk 19:5). Zacchaeus was overjoyed at this invitation, and when others started grumbling about Jesus' choice of dinner host, Zacchaeus spontaneously announced some remarkable resolutions: "Look, half of my possessions,

Lord, I will give to the poor; and if I have defrauded anyone of anything, I will pay back four times as much" (Lk 19:8).

Jesus treated people with the utmost respect. For him there were no social classes or status requirements, no "us and them." All people—young and old, men and women, co-nationals and foreigners—they were all precious to him. In his person, he fulfilled St. Paul's words that "there is no longer Greek and Jew, circumcised and uncircumcised, barbarian, Scythian, slave and free" (Col 3:11). His heart embraced them all.

What evidence is there in my life experience that Jesus "passionately desires my company"?

This is consoling because it means that his heart also embraces me. No matter who I am and what qualities (and defects) I possess, he wants me by his side. He longs to have me with him for all eternity. As incomprehensible as it may seem, he passionately desires my company. It also means that I can announce his love to every single person, with the absolute confidence that he loves them, too.

This universal heart poses a real challenge to us who follow Jesus. It is terribly hard to love everyone, especially those who appear so downright unlovable. Yet not to do so means to introduce a rift between our hearts and his. Only by loving each and every one, and desiring their eternal salvation, can we attain the union with Christ that we long for.

Lord, thank you for welcoming everyone and for giving me such a striking example of openness. You looked right past appearances and cut to the core of people, finding good in each one of them. You saw not only what they were but also what they could be. And this gaze of love and encouragement brought out the best in people.

You bring out the best in me, too, Lord. When I walk into a church or chapel where you are present, I feel at home. I feel welcome. It's true that when I've done something wrong I feel ashamed and unclean, and I sometimes wonder whether you look at me that way. But deep down, I know that you don't. You always want me with you. Your love gives me the courage to get up again, to try harder, to love more.

Help me to be this way with other people. Give me eyes to see them the way you see them, to overlook their faults and disagreeableness in order to find the good and the beautiful. My heart should exclude no one, just as yours didn't.

———◆◆◆———

Heart of Jesus, universal in its love for all,
make my heart more like yours!

JUNE 25

A **magnanimous** HEART

"Love your enemies."
Lk 6:27

The universality of Christ's heart went to the extreme of even loving those who hated him and wished him ill. He never repaid evil with evil but always responded with good. Most of us grew up hearing that Christians were supposed to love their enemies, so we can forget how genuinely novel and ground-breaking this teaching and behavior was.

One of the characteristics of Christian love is its superiority to mere justice, considered by Greek philosophers the great-

Why do we find it so difficult to love our enemies?

est of the virtues. Justice disposes us to give others their due, which already sets a high standard for human conduct. Many times, we don't go that far. But Jesus raised the bar higher still. "For if you love those who love you, what reward do you have? Do not even the tax collectors do the same?" (Mt 5:46-47). In other words, just giving people what they deserve doesn't make one a Christian. Returning love for love (strict justice) reflects a merely human standard. It is in loving those who do not love us that we show ourselves to be truly Christian and Christlike.

This was what Jesus practiced. Imagine what it was like for him to travel and eat every day with Judas Iscariot, who he knew would betray him for thirty pieces of silver? He treated him with the same kindness, the same respect, and the same friendship that he showed the other apostles. He showed him the honor of appointing him treasurer of the group, a position of trust. At the Last Supper, he even washes his feet. Similarly, Jesus accepts the acclamations of the crowds on Palm Sunday, fully aware that many of these same people would be crying out for his crucifixion a few days later. And with his dying breaths from the cross he prays to his Father to forgive his executioners, "for they do not know what they are doing" (Lk 23:34).

In a real way, all of us have directly benefited from this. We were all God's "enemies." St. Paul writes with the deepest appreciation: "But God proves his love for us in that while we still were sinners Christ died for

What do you think Jesus' top three priorities are, and where would "loving one's enemies" fit into them?

us" (Rom 5:8). He notes that "rarely will anyone die for a righteous person—though perhaps for a good person someone might actually dare to die" (Rom 5:7). It's truly astonishing that "while we were enemies, we were reconciled to God through the death of his Son" (Rom 5:10).

So when Jesus tells his disciples: "Love your enemies" and "Pray for your persecutors" (Mt 5:44), he knows full well what he is asking of them. He has felt in his own flesh how hard this is, and knows what it means to will only good to the very one who is seeking with all his might to harm you.

Jesus' example has inspired many others in the history of Christianity. The first martyr, the deacon St. Stephen, was stoned to

Have I ever witnessed someone I know truly loving their enemies?

death and was heard to cry out, "Lord, do not hold this sin against them" (Acts 7:60).

The 20th-century saint, Maria Goretti, likewise forgave her killer, Alessandro Serenelli. She died shortly before her twelfth birthday in 1902. Alessandro, who had stabbed Maria fourteen times because she would not give in to his advances, later repented and attended her canonization ceremony in 1950. If you are old enough you may remember the touching scene of Pope John Paul II visiting his would-be assassin, Mehmet Ali Agca in prison in 1983. Agca had shot and nearly killed the Pope in May 1981 in St. Peter's Square.

Most of us don't have "enemies" per se, so it may be difficult to understand how this injunction applies to us. But "enemies"

If I were to die today and go before God's judgment seat, and if God were to ask me, "Did you love your enemies?" how would I answer?

here refers to anyone who would seem to have no claim on our love, especially those whom we judge to deserve bad treatment.

Any time we have been cheated or betrayed, any time a friend, spouse, brother or sister has let us down, any time we have been judged harshly or spoken to unkindly, we have the opportunity to "love our enemies." It is precisely when the other least deserves our love that we are directed to give it. In this way, we imitate the abundance and gratuitousness of God's love.

Lord Jesus, your example of magnanimity astounds and moves me. You never set limits on your love. You never asked, "Isn't that enough?" or "Hey, that's not fair." For you, there were no limits and no bounds. You were willing to do anything, give anything, suffer anything to save us.

Thank you for this generosity. I may not have believed it was possible if you hadn't done it first. You have shown me—both in dealing with me and with others—that the only true love is a love without qualifications, conditions or restrictions. Thank you for not treating me as I deserve. Thank you for going beyond strict justice and for loving me when I least deserved it.

Help me to start today by showing love to those who have treated me poorly. Let me forget the wrongs done to me and love my "enemies" as you loved yours. Let me begin by willing good for them, especially the greatest good: their salvation.

———•◦•◦•———

Jesus, magnanimous of heart,
make my heart more like yours!

JUNE 26

A eucharistic HEART

"This is my body."
Lk 22:19

The essence of love is self-donation. We become a gift for another person and allow him or her to dispose of us as they see fit. Jesus said that the greatest love a person can have is to lay down his life for his friends. This "laying down" of one's life can be literal or figurative, but in Jesus' case, it was absolutely literal.

On the night before he suffered, we read, Jesus was at supper with his disciples. He took bread, said the blessing, broke the bread, and gave it to them, saying, "This is my body, which is given for

167

How deep is my faith in and devotion to the Eucharist? What does the Eucharist really mean to me on a day-by-day, week-by-week basis?

you" (Lk 22:19). He took his life in his hands and delivered it over to his apostles. He became their food, their sustenance, their Eucharist. Prefiguring the death he would suffer the following day, Jesus offered his body and blood in sacrifice to God and also as the bread of angels.

What was Jesus thinking as he held up that bread and distributed it to those around him? What was going on in his heart? What memories came rushing through his mind? What hopes and desires? It was most certainly an act of love. He was giving himself as totally and perfectly as a human being can. He wanted to be there for his disciples—for all of us—in this moment and throughout the centuries. He wanted to be our comfort, our strength, our consolation, our home.

As central as this act was for all of Jesus' life, it wasn't disconnected from the rest. It was, rather, the culmination of a life of self-offering that began with the Incarnation. Consequently, when Christ came into the world, he said,

"Sacrifices and offerings you have not desired, but a body you have prepared for me... I have come to do your will, O God" (Heb 10:5, 7). The whole reason for coming into the world was to offer himself up. Jesus had a Eucharistic heart, a heart offered up continually for the Father and for those around him. Jesus didn't spare fatigue, hardships, travels, misunderstandings, and betrayals—anything as long as it could be of service for us, his friends. Whatever the cost, Jesus didn't hold back.

Jesus had taught that in order to bear fruit, a grain of wheat had to fall to the earth and die (see Jn 12:24). Only in giving

How would I define Christian love to a nonbeliever?

himself does a person truly begin to live and to give life to others. This was not a "rule" to be followed; Jesus was simply describing the nature of love. Love "dies" to itself and puts the other in the first place. In love, there is no self-seeking. Rather, as Paul writes, love "does not insist on its own way; it is not irritable or resentful; it does not rejoice in wrongdoing, but rejoices in the truth. It bears all things, believes all things, hopes all things, endures all things. Love never ends" (1 Cor 13:5-8). We see every one of these facets of love in the Eucharist.

What about us? We aren't called to redeem the world from its sin, but we are called to "walk just as he walked" (1 Jn 2:6). Our "attitude should be the same as that of Christ Jesus" (Phil 2:5 NIB), and we are invited to come "to the measure of the full stature of Christ" (Eph 4:13). That means having a Eucharistic heart like his. At the Last Supper, after he had washed the disciples' feet, Jesus said: "I have set you an example, that you also should do as I have done to you" (Jn 13:15). The love he has shown us is the love that we are to bear toward one another.

What relationships or situations in my life make for regular opportunities to "be Eucharistic"?

The Eucharist is service. It is humility. It is sacrifice. It is self-gift. If we are attentive, we will find that we have numerous opportunities to be Eucharistic with one another, to participate in Jesus' Eucharistic heart. In his encyclical letter *Deus Caritas Est,* Pope Benedict wrote that sometimes the most effective evangelization is performed without words: "A Christian knows when it is time to speak of God and when it is better to say nothing and to let love alone speak. He knows that

God is love and that God's presence is felt at the very time when the only thing we do is to love" (no. 31c).

Lord Jesus, I feel very spoiled. I partake of the banquet of your love so often, and yet I rarely appreciate what is really happening. I rarely thank you as you deserve for this glorious gift. How many times have I received your sacred body and blood, which you offered for my salvation? It's so easy to take your love and your sacrifice for granted. I want to thank you now.

Yet I know, too, that the Eucharistic celebration is itself a perfect act of thanksgiving. The Psalmist asks: "What shall I return to the LORD for all his bounty to me?" And he provides the answer: "I will lift up the cup of salvation and call on the name of the Lord" (Ps. 116:12-13). Please, let me always attend Mass with this attitude!

Make me, Lord, into a gift for my brothers and sisters. Let me serve them truly, anticipating their needs and giving myself without reserve. It is an honor to do so in your name. In serv-

ing them, grant me a share in your heart, your sentiments, your dispositions.

Eucharistic heart of Jesus,
make my heart more like yours!

JUNE 27

A peaceful HEART

"My peace I give you."
Jn 14:27

Each Christmas Eve at the midnight Mass, we read from the Old Testament prophet Isaiah, who foretells of the coming Messiah. In the most dramatic prose, he describes the child to be born, listing his titles: "Wonder-Counselor, God-Hero, Father-Forever, Prince of Peace" (Is 9:6). When the angels announce Jesus' birth to the astounded shepherds, they again promise peace: "Glory to God in the highest heaven, and on earth peace among those whom he favors!" (Lk 2:14). One of the signs of the arrival of

A HEART LIKE HIS

the savior was to be a reign of peace, a time like that of Solomon, with prosperity and freedom from strife.

How deeply do I desire the peace God wants to bring into my life? How deeply do I believe that he can indeed bring it? The Hebrew greeting "Shalom," which Jesus repeats many times, carries richer connotations than our contemporary under-standing of "peace." More than just the absence of war and contention, it signifies the fullness of being, the presence of everything good, wholeness, health, and prosperity. But it also means harmony and concord among peoples. Jesus is the true Prince of Peace—the one who brings with him every-thing that is good.

At the Last Supper, Jesus offers his disciples a share in his own peace, a different sort than the world gives. "Peace I leave with you; my peace I give to you. I do not give to you as the world gives. Do not let your hearts be troubled, and do not let them be afraid" (Jn 14:27). Jesus removes our fears and fills us with his Holy Spirit, whose fruits St. Paul will enumerate as "love, joy, peace, patience, kindness, generosity, faithfulness, gentle-ness, and self-control" (Gal 5:22-23). Peace is both a choice and a gift. It is a choice, as love and trust in God bring peace to the heart. It is a gift, as Jesus offers us a sharing in his own perfect peace.

Which aspect of peace— peace as choice or peace as gift—do I need to pay more attention to?

Jesus truly had a peaceful heart. He was at peace with his Father, with humanity and with all creation. A soul at prayer is a soul at peace, and Jesus lived in constant contact with his Father. His trust was absolute, as was his loving, filial acceptance of the Father's will. The deepest sources of peace—trust, single-heartedness, generosity, openness to God's will—all character-ized the heart of Christ. He feared nothing, since he had the Father's love, which meant he had everything.

Jesus became our peace. He proclaimed the peacemakers to be blessed, "for they will be called children of God" (Mt 5:9). Yet he was himself the true peacemaker, the one who healed man's enmity with God. In Paul's words, "through him God was pleased to recon-cile to himself all things, whether on earth or in heaven, by making peace through the blood of his cross" (Col 1:20). The peace that matters most is the peace that Jesus won for us: peace with God. It is the beginning of any lasting peace between peoples.

When I think of "peace," do the images that come immediately to mind reflect better Christ's understanding of peace, or one of the false interpretations" of this peace?

It is true that Jesus warns against false interpretations of this peace. "Do not think that I have come to bring peace to the earth," he cautions. "I have not come to bring peace, but a sword" (Mt 10:34). Following Jesus will necessarily mean being a sign of contradiction. It will stir up animosity and incomprehension, even from family and friends. But the true peace he promises is not a superficial "getting along" with everybody, but the deeper peace that comes from communion with God and living in his love. This is the peace that Jesus himself possessed and lived. And so he tells his apostles that on the one hand, "in the world you face persecution" while on the other, to "take courage; I have conquered the world!" (Jn 16:33). And he teaches them all of this "so that in me you may have peace" (Jn 16:33).

As Christians seeking a heart like Christ's, we are called to live in peace and be builders of peace. By working for justice, by growing in trust in God, by casting out fear and anxiety, by detaching ourselves from aspirations that clash with the Father's will, by building bridges between people, by forgiving offenses, we become instruments and channels of Christ's peace, a peace the world cannot give. And we, too, receive the blessing of being called children of God.

Lord Jesus, Prince of Peace, blessed be your holy name! Thank you for giving me a share in your peace, a foretaste of the peace of heaven where every tear will be wiped dry, where sadness will be banished and where perfect harmony will reign. When I am with you, all the cares and worries of a lifetime seem to melt away. You are a sweet balm of peace for my soul. All I ask is that you never let me be separated from you. When I have you, I have everything.

Grant me, Lord, a peaceful heart. Your will is my peace. In loving submission to your plan for my life, I find the peace and joy of fulfillment. Often, I am the cause of my own anxiety and unrest. Teach me to let go of everything outside of your will for me.

St. Francis asked that you make him a channel of your peace. I ask the same thing. Let me bring your peace to a world that suffers from suspicion, distrust, and the pain of millennia of wars and betrayals. Let me bring peace to my family and my community. Let me bring peace to my friends and coworkers. Help me not to settle for the false peace of flattery and people-pleasing, but the deeper peace of justice, truth and reconciliation.

Jesus, peaceful of heart,
make my heart more like yours!

JUNE 28

A patient HEART

"Put your finger in my side."
Jn 20:27

More than once, Jesus manifested exasperation because of the lack of faith of those who approached him. His response to the crowds when his disciples failed to cure an epileptic boy is memorable: "You faithless and perverse generation, how much longer must I be with you? How much longer must I put up with you?" (Mt 17:17). When the Pharisees and Sadducees ask for a sign from heaven, Jesus says, "An evil and adulterous generation asks for a sign, but no sign will be given to it except the sign of Jonah" (Mt 16:4). Every day, Jesus worked signs and wonders, but for some, it never seemed to be enough.

How much do I value the virtue of patience in my friends, family members, and coworkers?

Through all this, however, Jesus revealed a remarkably patient heart. In his celebrated list of the qualities of Christian love, St. Paul places "patience" in the first place. "Love is patient. Love is kind. Love is not envious or boastful or arrogant or rude..." (1 Cor 13:4-5). This is a perfect description of Christ's own heart. He was truly patient, putting up with things that few of us would have the forbearance to endure: slowness of understanding, resistance to God's grace, lessons unlearned, worldly standards, pettiness, jealousy, and betrayal.

This patience is especially evident with his chosen disciples. He bears with their foibles and silly questions. He accepts their human weaknesses and flaws. Even his reproaches are filled with tenderness and compassion, like his "rebuke" of Peter after he panics while attempting to walk across the water to Jesus: "Man of little faith, why did you doubt?" (Mt 14:31). Jesus chose to work with imperfect instruments when he could perfectly well have done things better and faster himself. He continues to do so today, which means our own limitations are never an excuse to say no to his invitations.

After the Resurrection, the examples of this patience continue. The two disciples of Emmaus abandon all hope after the death of Jesus and decide to return to their homes (see Lk 24:13-35). Ever the Good Shepherd, Jesus doesn't simply let them leave but rather goes out to meet them on the road, patiently explaining the Scriptures to them and all the prophecies that foretold that the Messiah had to suffer and so enter into his glory. Again, his gentle reproach, "How foolish you are, and how slow of heart to believe all that the prophets have declared!" (Lk 24:25), is clothed in mildness and love.

Perhaps the greatest example of this patience is Jesus' encounter with the apostle Thomas, who has doggedly refused to believe in Jesus' resurrection: "Unless I see the mark of the nails in his hands, and put my finger in the mark of the nails and my hand in his side, I will not believe" (Jn 20:25). Jesus could easily have left Thomas to his own devices. "Fine, if that's the way he wants it," Jesus could have said, "let him persist in his unbelief." But he doesn't. He condescends to Thomas'

Do I tend to be as patient with others as I would like them to be with me? Why or why not?

weakness and fulfills his demands. When he appears to the Eleven, he says to Thomas, "Put your finger here and see my hands. Reach out your hand and put it in my side. Do not doubt but believe" (Jn 20:27).

Which of the seven sacraments do you think most eloquently illustrates the patience of the Heart of Christ? Why?

Each of us has experienced the patient love of Christ firsthand. How many times have we failed him in matters little and great, and yet he does not give up on us. How long he has had to wait for us to come around or respond to his grace, and yet, he has waited! How many times he could have justifiably thrown in the towel with us, looking for more faithful, qualified coworkers, and yet he has not!

Jesus' patience is a marvelous lesson for us Christians, who can get so frustrated with others' failings. When others seem to slow us down, when people don't "get it," when we feel let down by someone we counted on, we must remember Christ—the way he treated his disciples and the way he has dealt with us. We all must bear one another's crosses at times, knowing that others have often borne ours.

Lord Jesus, how great is your patience! You surrounded yourself with common men and women, bearing with their defects, limitations, and human failings. You could have at least chosen qualified professionals to found your Church, but you didn't. You chose fishermen and tax collectors—rude, uneducated men. What an example you give me of patience and forbearance!

In this, at least, I am like the apostles. I, too, am frail and full of flaws. You have chosen me to be your disciple, your evangelizer, your co-worker, knowing full well of my many faults and weaknesses. You didn't choose me for my qualities or my talents, so that the power of your grace would shine through my human weakness. I have failed you many times, yet you never give up on me. You never send me away. Thank you for being so patient with me—let me be worthy of your patience!

Teach me, Lord, to be patient with those around me. Remind me often of how patient you have had to be with me, so that I don't presume to be more severe with others than you have been with me. Patience is the first trait of love, and you know I want to love as you do.

Jesus, patient of heart,
make my heart more like yours!

JUNE 29

A **heavenly** HEART

"Where your treasure is, there will your heart be."
Lk 12:34

St. Paul famously distinguished between those who "live by the flesh" and those who live "according to the spirit" (see especially Rom 8). Those who live by the flesh, Paul suggested, are interested primarily in worldly things (things of the flesh), while those who live by the spirit "set their minds on things of the spirit." The flesh and the spirit war against one another, each trying to get the upper hand in our hearts, souls, and lives.

Where does the tension between being interested in worldly things and being interested in godly things usually make itself seen in my daily life?

Each of us experiences this battle. It is often easier to get excited about frivolities than about things that really matter. The spiritual life seems to require more work than planning parties or sporting events. We may sometimes get distracted at prayer thinking about a party, but we rarely get distracted during a party thinking about prayer. Jesus, on the other hand, was decidedly a man of the spirit. He saw things in a spiritual way, evaluated things from a spiritual perspective, and related things to deeper, spiritual truths.

When Jesus walked through the fields, for example, and saw the workers harvesting, he didn't just think about wheat and bread. He didn't lecture his disciples on good agricultural practice. He spontaneously thought that in supernatural terms, "the harvest is great and the laborers are few," and he encouraged his followers to "pray the Lord of the harvest to send workers to his harvest" (Mt 9:37-38). He thought about the harvest at the end of the world, when God's angels will separate the children of God from the children of the evil one, the way reapers separate wheat from chaff (Mt 13:36-

43). His thoughts tended upward, not downward. Earthly realities reminded him of heavenly realities.

On a typical day, how often do I spontaneously think about the heavenly meaning of earthly realities?

But this is the way Jesus always saw things, isn't it? Everything seemed to remind him of his Father and bear the fingerprints of the Creator of all. When he saw women rejoicing over a lost coin that had been refound or shepherds diligently seeking a sheep that had strayed, he was reminded that there is more rejoicing in heaven over a repentant sinner than over many who had no need to repent. When he heard about pearl merchants who had found and purchased an especially valuable pearl, he immediately thought of how the kingdom of heaven was like that pearl: precious and worth selling everything. When he saw the lilies of the field or the ravens of the air, he marveled at how his Father cared for all his creation and drew the lesson that we need not worry about insignificant things. Over and over again, simple, day-to-day occurrences made Jesus think of God, heaven, and eternal truths.

Jesus was truly the opposite of a "man of the world." He was a man of heaven, a man who saw everything supernaturally, a man

In a typical week, how many conversations do I have about spiritual topics? How many do I have about worldly topics?

for whom only eternal truths were really interesting. He could care less about gossip, who was in power, politics, or the social affairs of his time. He didn't get excited about sports teams or economic markets or the movements of Roman troops. He cared about people and especially about their relationship with God. He cared about big questions, transcendent questions, spiritual questions.

Even when four men brought Jesus a paralyzed man lying on a stretcher and laid him down before him, his thoughts went to spiritual questions. Instead of merely attending to the man's physical needs, Jesus' first thought was to heal his soul. "My child, your sins are forgiven" (Mk 2:5, NJB). He only cured his physical ailment as an afterthought, as proof that he had the power to forgive sins. Jesus first saw a person's soul, and only afterward the body. His real concern was for a person's interior well-being. He perfectly fulfilled the words of the prophet Samuel: "The Lord does not see as mortals see; they look on the outward appearance, but the Lord looks on the heart" (1 Sam 16:7).

Lord, you have chosen me to live in the world without being of the world. You don't want me to disdain the beautiful things you have created, but you also don't want me to set my heart on them. You teach me that the world as we know it is passing away, and that my true home is heaven. Even though I know these things, I am still in many ways a worldly person. Spiritual realities can seem very abstract to me, and worldly realities seem more tangible. It's true that my heart often naturally tends toward lower things and is attracted by more superficial interests rather than deeper, spiritual things.

What a wonderful example you give me of what it means to live as a spiritual person! Your priorities were always clear, and you always placed eternal truths above earthly concerns. You had a beautiful way of relating all things to higher truths, and so all of creation became a window to your Father. Thank you for being a model for me of how to think and act spiritually, with a heavenly heart.

Teach me, Lord, to think and act like you. Help me be a person of faith, who sees God's hand in everything. Help me go beyond appearances to look into the heart of people and events, and help me to care more for people's eternal good than simply for their momentary well-being. In short, help me to become more spiritual!

Heavenly heart of Jesus,
make my heart more like yours!

june 30

A wise HEART

"Man does not live by bread alone."
Lk 4:4

St. Paul incisively distinguished between the wisdom of the world, and true Christian wisdom. "God's foolishness," he wrote, "is wiser than human wisdom, and God's weakness is stronger than human strength" (1 Cor 1:25). The Christian understanding of wisdom goes beyond mere cleverness, education, or data accumulation. Indeed, this worldly, two-dimensional sort of

When I think of the word "wisdom," what images, memories, or concepts come immediately to mind? Why?

wisdom merely "puffs up," without building anything lasting (see 1 Cor 8:1). Christian wisdom goes beyond mere facts and information. It deals with *meaning* and with *value*. This is the wisdom that Jesus possessed in abundance.

Jesus often spoke about the worth of things, their eternal value. He encouraged his followers to abandon the frenetic search for worthless things in order to pursue true treasures. This was wisdom. Wisdom—according to Pope Benedict—seeks to understand *what matters*. Whereas knowing many things may be useful, it is nothing without wisdom. Wisdom, says Benedict, "is knowledge of the essential, knowledge of the aim of our life and of how we should live" (Homily, August 30, 2009).

How many times Jesus warns the wealthy that their riches will not save them! He encourages them to store up another sort of treasure, one that lasts forever. How many times does Jesus explain that merely temporal goods are nothing when compared to eternal ones! Even regarding our physical lives, he enjoins us not to fear those who kill the body but cannot kill the soul (Mt 10:28). In the end, it is the soul that matters. This, too, is wisdom. Not the dime-store wisdom ladled out by pundits and pragmatists, but the real wisdom that sees as God sees.

When tempted by Satan to turn stones into loaves, Jesus does not deny the importance of food, or the fact that he was hungry and would have gladly filled his belly with bread. Rather, Jesus underscores the insufficiency of material bread, and indeed all material gains. "Man does not live on bread alone," he remarked, "but on every word that comes forth from the mouth of God" (Mt 4:4). Yes, bread is good, but ultimately unsatisfying. God's word fills not the stomach but the heart and soul.

Jesus' heart was wise, not just because he possessed a bounty of knowledge but because he understood the worth of things. He immedi-

Do I tend to value things and people the way Jesus did, or the way popular culture does? Why?

ately saw what mattered and distinguished it from what was unimportant or useless. He praised the gift of a poor widow, appraising its value beyond that of the hefty donations of the wealthy. He declared the meek, the humble, and the poor in spirit to be blessed, while admonishing the proud, the self-confident, and the worldly wise. He commended those whose actions were good and revealed the emptiness of mere talk (see Mt 7:21-27). He saw value in purity, in innocence, in goodness, in service, and in many other qualities that the wise of this world scoff at as irrelevant.

> *If an outside observer of my life were to make a list of the three things that I value most, what would they come up with?*

Once again, one of the most compelling aspects of Jesus' teaching is the way it is reflected in his own life. Jesus' own scale of values mirrored the lessons he offered to the crowds. He lived simply, humbly, purely, temperately, with his heart placed firmly in heaven. He didn't counsel one sort of life and live another. He knew that words without actions were mere "lip service," to be blown away with the wind.

Christ's teaching and witness of wisdom proves particularly consoling to those whose lives are filled with thousands of daily chores and little opportunity for ongoing education and academic pursuits. Christian wisdom is accessible to everyone, from the taxi driver to the dentist to the firefighter to the shop clerk. Paying attention to what matters and disregarding what doesn't requires no PhD but fills the heart with a wisdom surpassing that of the learned and the clever.

Lord, you never went to college, and yet, you are the teacher of humanity. At the age of twelve, you were already sitting amongst the doctors. Your wisdom transcends the brilliance of scientists and the expertise of professionals, since you possessed the only knowledge that will matter in the end: knowledge of God and the meaning of human existence. You taught in the simplest way—with stories and parables—yet the knowledge you conveyed mattered more than entire libraries of scholarship.

I take pride in my education and like to appear well schooled, yet in your eyes this matters very little. Help me to adjust my way of thinking to yours. Let me appreciate the wisdom of small children and senior citizens and salt-of-the-earth neighbors whose common sense and eternal perspective makes them wise like you. Let me seek not only knowledge but also wisdom to distinguish what matters from what doesn't.

Praised be your holy name, dear Jesus! You knew where true value lay, and pursued it alone. You didn't allow human approval to color your evaluation of things, but looked only to your Father to set your goals and priorities. Teach me to be wise like you. Teach me not only what is, but why it is and what it means.

--------◆◆◆◆--------

Wise heart of Jesus,
make my heart more like yours!

additional meditations

The following meditations can be substituted for the ordinary scheduled meditations on the Solemnity of the Sacred Heart of Jesus, and the following day on the Feast of the Immaculate Heart of Mary.

solemnity of the
sacred heart of jesus

A loving HEART

*"The Word became flesh
and lived among us."*

Jn 1:14

If the human heart symbolizes anything, it symbolizes love. We draw hearts on Valentine cards and carve them into tree bark, signifying our love for that special other. In American sign language, you express love by crossing both hands over your heart. Jesus' heart, too, despite its many other qualities and virtues, stands above all for his love. Put another way, all the other qualities and virtues we have been consid-

When I think about Christ's love for me, do my thoughts correspond to a personal, deeply felt experience, or an abstract concept?

ering in the pages of this book are really so many facets of Christ's love.

The solemnity of the Sacred Heart celebrates Christ's overwhelming love for mankind, and for each of us in particular. It is an especially intimate feast, since it focuses on Christ's interior life and his personal relationship with each one of us. The biblical expression "God so loved the world that he sent his only son" could be faithfully reworded "Jesus Christ so loved the world that he took flesh, lived, and died for me." In Paul's words, Christ "loved me and gave himself for me" (Gal 2:20). Christ's love is personal, passionate, enduring, heroic, and eternal. Today is a day to contemplate that love, experience that love, and respond to that love.

Spiritual writers through the centuries have rightly noted that the beginning of love is the experience of being loved. We love because we have been loved. We have experienced love from our parents and family, but above all from God himself, who is the source of all true love. This is why St. John could write, "This is love: not that we loved God, but that he loved us"

(1 Jn 4:10, NIV). The more truly we realize and feel and know this love, the more naturally we love in return.

When we read God's Word, we should form the habit of looking not just at Jesus' words and actions—the story of his life. On every page, we

Take a few moments to give a complete answer to one of these questions, an answer that really resonates in the depths of your soul.

should stop and ask ourselves *why*. Why the Incarnation? Why the birth in a poor stable in Bethlehem? Why the flight into Egypt? Why the presentation in the temple? Why the hidden years at Nazareth? Why the baptism in the Jordan? Why three years of teaching, healing, traveling, and serving? Why the Last Supper? Why the agony in the garden? Why the Passion? Why the Cross? Why the Resurrection? The answer to these and all the other whys of Christ's life is always the same: because he loved me. He *loves* me. And he would do it all over again a thousand times for me.

Every page of the Gospel is a testament to Jesus' love for me. It is a love letter, and I am its unworthy recipient. Do you ever think that when Jesus was doing all those things he was already thinking of you? He had you in his mind and heart. Do you ever think as you read your Bible that Jesus knew you would be reading it, that it is truly written for you? It didn't fall into your hands by chance, and you aren't snooping around someone else's diary. It was intended for you.

Is there by chance something in me that resists accepting this personal, passionate, unconditional love of Jesus for me? If so, what is it? What would Jesus say about it?

There is another side of the coin to Jesus' love for you, and that is your response. This is the second half of this great feast. When revealing his heart to her, Jesus said to St. Margaret Mary Alacoque: "Behold the Heart that has so loved men . . . instead of gratitude I receive from the greater part of mankind only ingratitude." It is truly heartbreaking to think of the indifference to this love of so many cold hearts, especially when we realize that our own hearts are often indifferent to it. The idea of *reparation* to the heart of Jesus begins with this sorrowful acknowledgement and continues by a sincere effort to respond to love with love.

What a difference it would make in our lives if we simply lived with an ongoing awareness of God's love for us! This awareness could not leave us indifferent but necessarily would inspire gratitude. To contemplate the heart of Jesus is to contemplate his

What can I do to remind myself throughout the day that Jesus really does know me and love me deeply and personally?

love. We praise him. We thank him. We offer him our own poor love, which he so desperately desires.

Dearest Jesus, words cannot adequately express my gratitude for your love. Thank you, thank you for your love for me. Thank you for becoming man for me and for living and dying for me. Let me never forget this. Let me never become hardened to this central truth of my entire existence. You love me! No matter what befalls me, no matter what direction my life takes, you will always be there with your love for me. You will be my strength, my consolation, my all.

I trust in your love. You spared nothing to show me your love. No sacrifice was too big for you, no cross too heavy. What could you possibly deny me? If I have your love, I have everything. You will be there for me, in good times and in bad, in darkness and in light, in trials and in joys.

Jesus, I love you so much. You better than anyone know how poor and fragile my love is, yet I wish it were a bonfire like your own. I desire to love you more, to love you as you deserve. I wish to be an apostle of your love, to help others to know and experience it, so that they may love you, too. Please grant me this desire.

———◦✦◦———

Heart of Jesus, burning bonfire of love,
make my heart more like yours!

feast of
the immaculate
heart of mary

A **MARIAN** HEART

"Behold your mother."
Jn 19:27

One of the truly amazing aspects of Jesus' relationship with Mary, his mother, was their uncanny ability to understand each other with very few words. Though they must have had many long conversations, those recorded in the Gospels are brief, almost cryptic. It seems that they knew each other so well that words were practically superfluous.

Perhaps without intending it, Mary was the catalyst for Jesus' first miracle: the conversion of water into wine at Cana in

Galilee. When Mary realizes that the wine has run out and that the marriage banquet is about to take a sobering turn, she turns to Jesus. Yet she doesn't offer any long explanations of the couple's embarrassing situation. She doesn't detail the consequences of this miscalculation or appeal to Jesus' filial love. She doesn't beg or entreat; in fact, she doesn't even make a request. She merely states with remarkable economy of expression: "They have no wine" (Jn 2:3). And Jesus responds with similar brevity, "Woman, what concern is that to you and to me? My hour has not yet come" (Jn 2:4). Taking that as a "yes" (where you and I would have heard "no"), Mary says nothing more to her son but turns to the servants and instructs them to "do whatever he tells you" (Jn 2:5). The result is Jesus' first "sign."

Whenever I meet someone's parents for the first time, I am almost always struck by the resemblances. Sometimes they are physical—the nose, the eyes, the shape of the jaw—but still more often they are found in recognizable gestures—a tilt of the head, a scrunch of the nose, a characteristic motion of the hands. Without realizing it, we assimilate an awful lot from the people we spend most time with. After spending thirty years living with Mary, Jesus surely resembled her in numerous ways.

The disciples would have picked these up at once, and after Jesus'
resurrection, her presence in their midst was a constant reminder
of her son.

But of all the ways Mary was
like Jesus, surely the deepest and most characteristic
of all was in the heart. Jesus
was her beloved son, and he

*In what ways is Mary
present "in my midst"
the way she was with
the Apostles after Jesus'
Ascension?*

was also her God. She learned from him even as he learned
from her. In St. Luke's Gospel, where we learn the most about
Mary, we read not once but twice a striking phrase describing Mary's heart. Luke describes her as profoundly contemplative and spiritual. Shortly after Jesus' birth, Mary, Joseph,
and their newborn son are visited by shepherds, who tell of a
vision of angels. For her part, Mary "treasured all these words
and pondered them in her heart" (Lk 2:19). She stored away
the marvelous memories of God's action in her life, turning
them over and over.

Later, when as a twelve-year-old Jesus stays behind at the
temple talking with the doctors, Jesus seems not to understand his parents' concern and responds with the enigmatic

Why do you think Mary treasured and pondered Jesus' words? What do I tend to "turn over and over" in my heart? Why?

rhetorical question: "Did you not know that I must be in my Father's house?" (Lk 2:49). He rejoins his parents and returns with them to Nazareth, where he was obedient to them. But once again, we find that Mary "treasured all these things in her heart" (Lk 2:51).

Like Jesus, Mary had a prayerful heart, a contemplative heart. She was not impetuous or superficial but thoughtful and profound. Like Jesus, Mary's heart was pure, undivided,

In what ways have I experienced the motherly love of Mary's heart in my own faith journey?

compassionate, merciful, patient, courageous, and all the other virtues we have considered in this volume. She was obedient as he was,

asking only that it "be done unto me according to your word" the way Jesus always prayed "not my will but yours be done."

She was deeply loving and considerate as well. When she learns that her elderly cousin Elizabeth is with child, she hastens off to attend to her needs—despite the fact that she has just found out that she herself is pregnant with the Savior of the world! No one mirrored Jesus' heart the way Mary did, and no one was more anxious to bring others to him than she was—and still is.

The Church reminds us of the singular union that exists between Mary and her son, especially through these back-to-back feasts. One day, we meditate on Jesus' Sacred Heart, and the next day, we consider Mary's immaculate heart. The same thing happens in September, when on the 14th we contemplate Jesus' passion on the feast of the Exaltation of the Cross, and the very next day is dedicated to Mary's sharing in the passion as Mother of Sorrows—mother and son can never be far apart.

Dearest Mary, thank you for your faithfulness to God's call. Thank you for embracing the angel Gabriel's message of salvation and agreeing to become the mother of the Redeemer. Thank you for staying true to God throughout your life and accompanying Jesus all the way through his passion. You are a model for me, as well as being my dear mother, given to me by Jesus from the cross. Hold my

hand as I try to do the same. Intercede for me, and pray that my heart may grow daily more like your Son's.

Lord Jesus, few people on earth had the honor of being your teachers. Only one had the honor of being your mother—the woman you chose for this exceptional vocation. You loved her in a singular way, as only a son can love his mother. But you have made me your brother, and you have given me Mary to be my mother. Thank you for this generous gift. Help me to be worthy of this sublime dignity.

Jesus, we all need intercessors, and we all need models of what it means to follow you. Thank you for the treasure of your saints, and especially for the Queen of Heaven, your mother Mary. Because she humbled herself as the "handmaid of the Lord," you exalted her. Let me imitate her heart, so that I may also become more like you.

Marian heart of Jesus,
make my heart more like yours!

appendices

DEVOTION TO THE SACRED HEART OF JESUS

Devotion to the Sacred Heart is not separate from devotion to Jesus himself but is a part of it. It places special emphasis on Jesus' passionate love for human beings, represented by his human heart. In symbolic language, the heart represents the core of the person and is the seat of decisions, virtues, emotions, and, above all, love. Since God is love, Jesus Christ is love incarnate—*love made man*—and devotion to his Sacred Heart focuses on this essential dimension of Jesus. In Pope Benedict's words, "It is precisely through the heart of Jesus that the love of God for humanity is sublimely manifested." The devotion depicts Jesus' heart as wounded, pierced by a sword, encircled with a crown of thorns, and afire with love. It is tied, therefore, to devotion to Jesus' passion and death, and it underscores the love of Christ that permeated his self-donation on the cross for the salvation of humankind.

This devotion does not consist in a single act or acts; it consists especially in *returning love for love*. It means contemplating the great love Jesus has for us, growing in gratitude for this love, and trying to respond to it with our own love for him. It assumes a character of reparation, since Jesus reveals his Sacred Heart as sorrowing and treated with contempt and indifference. It also involves an active effort to get to know Jesus better in order to love him and imitate him more perfectly.

Devotion to the Sacred Heart grew especially out of a series of visions experienced by a French nun named Margaret Mary of Alacoque (1647-1690), a Visitation sister at the monastery of Paray-le-Monial. Obviously, devotion to Jesus' love for man did not begin there. St. John speaks of God so loving the world as to give his only son to be its savior (see Jn 3:16). St. Paul wrote: "I live by faith in the Son of God, who loved me and gave himself for me" (Gal 2:20). Devotion to the wounds of Christ focused especially on the wound in his side produced by the soldier's lance, and the blood and water that flowed from his open heart were seen by the Fathers of the Church as representing all the sacramental graces flowing to the Church from Jesus' heart.

Some saints of the middle ages, such as St. Mechtilde (d. 1298) and St. Gertrude (d. 1302) were especially dedicated to the heart of Christ, and this slowly grew into a fairly common "private devotion," especially as of the sixteenth century. It was St. Jean Eudes (1602-1680) who made the devotion "public," honoring it with an Office, and establishing a feast for it. But it was above all through Margaret Mary that this devotion was established and propagated throughout the universal Church.

Margaret Mary received numerous revelations. In 1673, on the feast of St. John the Evangelist, Jesus permitted Margaret Mary to rest her head upon his heart, and then revealed to her the wonders of his love, telling her that he desired to make them known to all mankind. He had chosen her for this work.

Jesus requested to be honored under the symbol of his heart of flesh and asked for a devotion of atoning love, with special emphasis on frequent reception of Holy Communion, Communion on the First Friday of each month, and the observance of the Holy Hour on Thursday evenings, in remembrance of the agony in the garden of Gethsemani.

During the octave of Corpus Christi, 1675, Margaret Mary received her "great apparition," when Jesus said to her: "Behold the Heart that has so loved men… instead of gratitude I receive from the greater part (of mankind) only ingratitude…" At this time, Jesus asked her for a feast of reparation to be celebrated on the Friday after the octave of Corpus Christi and told her to consult with her spiritual director, the Jesuit priest Father Claude de la Colombière (now a saint himself). Father de la Colombière believed in the authenticity of Margaret Mary's revelations and advised her to write an account of the apparition. For his part, Father de la Colombière became a zealous apostle of this devotion, consecrating himself to the Sacred Heart and propagating it wherever he could.

It wasn't until 1856, however, that the feast of the Sacred Heart of Jesus was extended to the universal Church by Pope Pius IX. Some forty years later, on June 11, 1899, Pope Leo XIII solemnly consecrated the entire world to the Sacred Heart, something which Leo would refer to as the "great act" of his pontificate. Leo, in fact, declared devotion to the Sacred Heart to be "the most acceptable form of piety" and said it would be "profitable to all."

Important papal encyclicals on devotion to the sacred Heart of Jesus

Pope Leo XIII, encyclical letter *Annum Sacrum*, May 25, 1899.

Pope Pius XI, encyclical letter *Miserentissimus Redemptor,* May 8, 1928

Pope Pius XI, encyclical letter *Caritate Christi Compulsi,* May 3, 1932.

Pope Pius XII, encyclical letter *Haurietis Aquas,* May 15, 1956.

promises of the sacred Heart

Specific devotions to the Sacred Heart became popular when St. Margaret Mary Alacoque had a personal revelation involving a series of visions of Christ as she prayed before the Blessed Sacrament. She wrote, "He disclosed to me the marvels of his love and the inexplicable secrets of his Sacred Heart." Included in these revelations were a series of promises. Jesus promised that, in response to those who consecrate themselves and make reparations to his Sacred Heart:

- *He will give them all the graces necessary in their state of life.*

- *He will establish peace in their homes.*

- *He will comfort them in all their afflictions.*

- *He will be their secure refuge during life, and above all, in death.*

- *He will bestow abundant blessings upon all their undertakings.*

- *Sinners will find in his heart the source and infinite ocean of mercy.*

- *Lukewarm souls shall become fervent.*

- *Fervent souls shall quickly mount to high perfection.*

- *He will bless every place in which an image of his heart is exposed and honored.*

- *He will give to priests the gift of touching the most hardened hearts.*

- *Those who shall promote this devotion shall have their names written in his heart.*

In the excessive mercy of his heart that his all-powerful love will grant to all those who receive Holy Communion on the First Fridays in nine consecutive months the grace of final perseverance; they shall not die in his disgrace, nor without receiving their sacraments. His divine heart shall be their safe refuge in this last moment.

The devotions attached to these promises are:

- *Receiving Communion frequently*

- *First Fridays: going to confession and receiving the Eucharist on the first Friday of each month for nine consecutive months. Many parishes will offer public First Friday devotions; if they do, you must perform First Fridays publicly. If it isn't so offered in your parish, you can do this privately, going to confession, receiving the Eucharist, and offering your prayers for the intention of the Holy Father.*

- *Holy Hour: Eucharistic Adoration for one hour on Thursdays ("Could you not watch one hour with me?"). Holy Hour can be made alone or as part of a group with formal prayers.*

- *Celebrating the Feast of the Sacred Heart*

enthronement of the sacred heart

Father Mateo Crawley-Boevey, a South American priest of the Congregation of the Sacred Hearts of Jesus and Mary, was inspired by God, after his instantaneous cure at Paray-le-Monial, to preach everywhere the Enthronement of the Sacred Heart to verify this promise of the Savior given to St. Margaret Mary: "I will bless every dwelling where an image of My Heart is both exposed and honored."

Enthronement of the Sacred Heart is a solemn act of a family giving formal recognition of the kingship of Christ over their family and home and the official, ceremonial beginning of a family's commitment to live out the effects of their recognition of Christ's kingship. During the Enthronement ceremony, a blessed image of the Sacred Heart is hung in the most prominent place in the house.